Francis Schaeffer's
APOLOGETICS:
A CRITIQUE

Francis Schaeffer's APOLOGETICS:

A CRITIQUE

By

Thomas V. Morris

MOODY PRESS

CHICAGO

© 1976 by
THE MOODY BIBLE INSTITUTE
OF CHICAGO

Library of Congress Cataloging in Publication Data

Morris, Thomas V
  Francis Schaeffer's apologetics.

  Bibliography: p. 126.
    1. Apologetics—20th century. 2. Schaeffer,
Francis August. I. Title.

BT1102.M69   239   75-43866

ISBN 0-8024-2873-8

Printed in the United States of America

Contents

Foreword

ONE OF THE CHIEF CRITICISMS popularly leveled against apologetics has been the charge that it settles for mere argumentative victory—as if convincing the unbeliever of the existence of God was, by itself, a significant achievement. To that tendency among apologists the teaching of John's gospel is relevant: the signs in John are offered, he declares, "that [men] might believe that Jesus is the Christ the Son of God *and* that believing [they] might have life through his name" (20:31).

An outstanding twentieth-century example of this combination of apologist and evangelist is Francis A. Schaeffer. Indeed, he has often publicly claimed to be nothing more than "an old time evangelist." Yet his presentation of Christianity, linked as it has been to the larger culture and to formal philosophy, has attracted the attention of academics in philosophy and apologetics.

Bertrand Russell on one occasion lamented that only "the fundamentalists and a few more learned Catholic theologians" could rouse him to dialectical fisticuffs, the rest of the world of religion having opted out of the debate. So Schaeffer, an orthodox Protestant, has earned a respectful hearing among skeptics and discriminating believers, not only for his gracious sensibilities but for the rational plausibility of his world view. This book concerns the latter.

Thomas Morris's analysis of Dr. Schaeffer's thought will serve the student of apologetics in at least four ways:

1. It shows where Schaeffer fits in the traditional schemes of philosophy of religion. There are, after all, many ways to do apologetics, ranging from the most austere presupposi-

tionalism to the most complex empiricism. Where is Francis Schaeffer on the spectrum? Morris's insight that the Schaeffer approach is a species of the argument from design is but one way the beginning student will feel on familiar ground.

2. The book will help students of modern apologetics discern the sense in which Schaeffer should be regarded a "presuppositionalist." In recent years there has been considerable debate over who among us is the most presuppositional of all. The variation seems to involve, first, the thing presupposed (is it logic? the Bible? the external world?); and second, the method for justifying it—that is, can anything be said on behalf of one's presuppositions that would make them a convincing starting point? Morris here shows both the content and method of Schaeffer's presuppositional apologetic.

3. While most of Schaeffer's apologetic activity has taken place in the intimacy of private dialogue, inevitably his message demands a response from the philosophical community. Philosophers traditionally have been in the business of appraising argument, weighing answers to the meaning of life, and pursuing the nature of reality. Schaeffer is therefore on philosophical ground (or, equally, philosophers are on theological ground), and some response is called for. Morris shows what a formal philosophical analysis of Schaeffer's apologetic would be like. We ought to bear in mind that the world of academic philosophy does not speak with one voice, and a critique of a Christian apologetic therefore could take many forms. But the author's academic background, with its rather cosmopolitan perspective, ensures that this critique is neither philosophically provincial nor eccentric.

4. Finally, Morris uncovers a nest of fascinating questions about the role of argument in religious faith. Technically, this is the relationship of philosophy of religion to psychology of religion. For example, why do people believe

in Christianity? And why do they do it with such intensity and certainty? To what extent is it a matter of a sound argument? Or is their faith a personal act that has next to nothing to do with good arguments or bad ones?

Of course, at this point apologetics rises above its academic context. For the reader, for Morris, for me, and eminently for Schaeffer himself, the intellectual reflection about Christianity is no parlor game. Schaeffer's influence has been most strongly felt among people who have gazed into the naturalistic abyss and have embraced despair. Whether from secular or religious backgrounds, they have listened to Schaeffer and his colleagues with the hope, if not the criterion, that a satisfying view of the universe must bear the marks of rationality.

The prevailing culture has been famished for meaning; the market has been bare—and within that marketplace the Meaning, the *Logos* of God, has been savingly reexamined. And in this way, twentieth-century people have not only believed but have found life through the meaningful Son of God.

STEPHEN BOARD

Introduction

FRANCIS AUGUST SCHAEFFER is one of the leading figures in what has been called "the evangelical renaissance." In 1948, after a ten-year pastorate in the United States, he went with his family to Switzerland as a missionary. In 1955, he and his wife began L'Abri Fellowship in the small town of Huemoz, Switzerland. Gradually, students travelling in Europe began to hear about L'Abri—that a man lived there who was relating orthodox biblical Christianity to contemporary culture and philosophical problems. In Schaeffer's own words:

> At L'Abri, I listened as well as talked. I learned something about twentieth-century thinking, in many fields, across many disciplines. Gradually, people began to come from the ends of the earth—not only students but professors. They heard that L'Abri was a place where one could discuss the great twentieth-century questions quite openly.
>
> To the best of my ability I gave the Bible's answers. But all the time I tried to listen and learn the thought forms of these people. I think that my knowledge, whatever it is, is formed from two factors: 1) 40 years of hard study, and 2) trying to listen to the twentieth-century man as he talked.[1]

So Dr. Schaeffer's work became international in its impact. He initially did not plan to write books or even tape-record his discussion sessions. But then someone taped one of his conversations, and requests were made for copies of the tape; thus a tape-program began which has grown to over a thousand hours of recorded lectures. These taped lectures, used at L'Abri by visiting students, are distributed around the world.

Dr. Schaeffer's first book, *The God Who Is There*, was published in 1968. It also had an unplanned genesis, appearing first as a pamphlet printed by Wheaton College students from a lecture he gave there. Since 1968, twenty more books have been published. His wife, Edith, has written four, and two of his closest associates at L'Abri (Os Guinness and Udo Middlemann) have recently published significant works. A flurry of books by other evangelical authors in areas of apologetics, theology, and general culture have also acknowledged Dr. Schaeffer's influence.

Thus, Schaeffer has become one of the most popular contemporary figures in evangelical Christian circles. Representative of this popularity is a quote from Eternity magazine:

> Francis A. Schaeffer is something of an evangelical phenomenon. Judging by the popularity of his books, he has more influence with today's youth—from members of the dropout world to the disillusioned heirs of evangelicalism—than any other one man.[2]

These books have been translated into fourteen different languages, with the English sales alone far exceeding two million volumes. Dr. Schaeffer states that

> the books all come from two sources: from the thousand-some hours of tapes and from our continuing discussions at L'Abri. We just sit around our fireplace and I kick off my shoes and talk and listen to the people who come there. And so the books have been kept up-to-date; they haven't yet become fixed.[3]

All of his books have a discussion or lecture format. They are all suggestive rather than carefully argumentative, and are written to reach a generally well-educated reading public. It is my opinion that Dr. Schaeffer is the modern, college-level counterpart of the old evangelical pamphleteer. His style and treatments are popular rather than philosophically rigorous so that he may reach a larger audience and have a more widespread effect on the church and the world.

In Part 1 of this study, I will attempt to analyze Dr. Schaeffer's major apologetic thrust—his presuppositional approach to theistic argumentation. After explicating and analyzing the individual argumentative formulations of his approach, I will offer some observations and evaluations concerning the intentions, methods, and results of his apologetic strategy as a whole. In Part 2, I will consider some very difficult but vital and practical questions which arise from my study. First, I will attempt to give a justification for the general type of apologetic enterprise in which both Dr. Schaeffer and I are involved, basing it on the way in which apologetic arguments can function in people's lives. Then I will sketch out very briefly how the valuable insights of Schaeffer's work may be appropriated and incorporated into a more complete Christian apologetic.

As a whole, this book is a philosophical study in the logic of apologetics. For this reason, theological and historical references have been kept to a minimum. I have tried to keep my arguments rigorous without making them overly technical. Underlying all these philosophical examinations is a firm commitment to the truth of Jesus' statement that "no one can come to Me, unless the Father who sent Me draws him" (John 6:44, NASB). It is only by the active grace of God that anyone believes as a Christian, but God often chooses human undertakings, such as apologetic arguments, as vehicles or instruments of that grace. Thus, there is value in examining how it is that human arguments can be related logically to Christian belief. That I have done in these pages.

Some of my ideas presented here (especially those in chapter 7) run against the grain of much contemporary philosophical and religious thought. However, two recently published books, which have come into my hands, move in the same general direction. For those readers who wish to pursue further some of the philosophical implications of my last chapters, I would suggest Basil Mitchell's *The Justification of Religious Belief* and Roger Trigg's *Reason and Commitment.* (Both are listed in the bibliography.)

Without the support of many friends, this book would be very different. I would like to thank Professors Jouett Powell and George Schlesinger for their encouragement during the time I worked on Part 1 in North Carolina, my colleagues in New Haven whose queries stimulated the writing of Part 2, and my wife, Mary, whose vital reminders and needed interruptions kept me functioning almost normally throughout the course of my work.

It is my desire that the critical analysis presented by this study will reveal both the values and the limits of argumentation such as Dr. Schaeffer's and consequently will contribute, if even in a small way, to what he himself has referred to as "the battle of our generation."

PART 1

The Apologetic Writings of Francis Schaeffer

1

The Pre-evangelistic, Presuppositional Argument

DR. SCHAEFFER'S BASIC APOLOGETIC APPROACH is to compare the presuppositions of orthodox reformed Christianity, "historic Christianity," with those of modern non-Christian world views. This is not undertaken by careful, formal analyses of rival philosophical positions, but by the application of generalized claims and criticisms in a pre-evangelism/evangelism scheme. "Pre-evangelism" is Schaeffer's term for the preparatory work necessary to bring a modern non-Christian to an awareness of his need for the evangel. The traditional sequence of evangelism has been to preach first law and judgment, and then grace and salvation. Schaeffer sees this as inadequate in itself to reach a great number of modern men whose presuppositions do not even allow the possibility of the supernatural or of divinely decreed moral absolutes, for example. Thus, Schaeffer has developed an apologetic strategy preliminary to the evangelical proclamation which challenges presuppositions alien to it.

Although the pre-evangelistic, presuppositional apologetic is set forth in *The God Who Is There* as necessary and indispensable in communicating with modern man, the nature of presuppositions is never clearly discussed. Schaeffer does not clarify what kinds of beliefs or propositions are to count as presuppositions, and are therefore to be examined by the apologist. Of course, a presupposition is an idea or concept which is assumed or posited in the manner of the premises of a deductive argument, itself unproven, but the first move toward other proofs which rest on it. The definition Schaeffer gives in a glossary is "a belief or theory which is assumed before the next step in logic is developed. Such a prior postulate often consciously or unconsciously affects the way a person subsequently reasons."[1]

The terminology in which Dr. Schaeffer casts this definition is noteworthy, as it indicates a tendency which will later be examined. The nouns "theory," "step," "logic," and "postulate" with the verb "to reason" give the definition a mathematical tone belying the nonmathematical nature of the definiendum. The reader is almost led to imagine men formulating syllogisms and proof lines over lunch. Surely the beliefs which are foundational to human life and underlie both the thoughts and actions of people are of a different genus than mathematical or otherwise formally deductive premises. Human presuppositions concerning life seem to be more like orientations toward existence and the world. The world picture (or pictures) of any individual is that which directs his thoughts, decisions, and actions. The recognition of an imaginative element to presuppositions in no way precludes the logical function which they can be said to perform. Whether a man dreams or reasons, he does so from a certain world picture, which Schaeffer calls a "set of presuppositions," however homogeneous or conglomerate it might be. Dreaming and reasoning, or further, the nonlogical and the logical, cannot finally be disjoined. Such a disjunction, when attempted, blurs and confuses important aspects of human thought. The point I want to make here as an aside (although it will be important further on) is that by his terminology and tone, Schaeffer is presenting a formalized or depersonalized view of human thought of which he himself seems not to be convinced but which permeates his philosophical apologetic discussions.

However, after giving the formal definitions of "presupposition," the question remains as to what kinds of ideas or concepts are to be considered presuppositions relevant to the apologist. It becomes clear in Schaeffer's books that one of the few foundational presuppositions of historic orthodox Christianity is the "infinite-personal" triune God. Accordingly, it has been said that he rejects the traditional proofs of the existence of God.[2] Although Schaeffer himself never mentions those proofs, one of his closest associates, Os Guinness, has explicitly repudiated theistic proof,[3] clearly revealing a position that the orthodox conception of God is not derivable from argumentation, but must be accepted from revelation and held presuppositionally. Thus argumentation may operate only in confirmatory or supporting roles, as is the manner of all presuppositional reasoning.

To the question of God, Schaeffer joins basic questions concerning the ultimate nature of the universe (including human phenomena) as the presuppositions foundational for any world view, which lie behind any orientation toward life, and which are therefore relevant to the Christian apologist. An important quote from one of his books will illustrate this:

> What I urge people to do is to consider the two great presuppositions—the uniformity of natural causes in a closed system and the uniformity of natural causes in an open system, in a limited time span—and to consider which of these fits the facts of what is.[4]

Schaeffer here asserts that, at bottom, there are only two possible basic presuppositions concerning the overall nature of the universe: that it is an autonomous, self-contained, random or self-regulated entity of matter-energy; or that there is a more basic reality than the physical universe which is a temporally limiting and spatially causing force in relation to that open system. To say that the universe is open is thus to say that it is open to something or Someone not identifiable with the universe; hence, the link between the question of God and questions of the universe.

The question of God and elementary questions of the ultimate nature of the universe are joined by Schaeffer into presuppositional sets and are considered jointly, consonant with basic belief-evaluation theory.[5] The method by which he presents the doctrines of historic Christianity for acceptance is first to posit the basic presuppositions. He then compares these presuppositions with their contradictories, and on the basis of explanatory power to subsume the data of human experience, argues the necessity of maintaining the orthodox Christian presuppositional set.

I want to define the terms "contradictory" and "contrary" as I will use them in evaluating Dr. Schaeffer's arguments. Any two sets of presuppositions, or more simply, any two statements, are contradictory if it can be said neither that both are true, nor that both are false. That is, if one of them is true, then the other must be false. They contradict each other. An example of a pair of contradictories is:

1. The world was created.
2. The world was not created.

If 1 is true then 2 must be false; if 2 is true then 1 must be false. They cannot both be true at the same time, nor can they both be false at the same time.

Any two sets of presuppositions or any two statements are said to be contrary if they cannot both be true but they can both be false. An example of a pair of contraries would be:

1. The world was created by the Greek god Zeus alone.
2. The world was created by the Norse god Thor alone.

Both 1 and 2 cannot be true at the same time, but both can be false—if, for example, it is true that the world was created by the God and Father of our Lord Jesus Christ. Later on I will try to show that, due to a failure to deal adequately with contraries to his position, the orthodox Christian position, Dr. Schaeffer does not succeed in demonstrating the necessity of that position, as he claims to have done. But his arguments do move in the direction of establishing its possibility, or even likelihood—a major move in the secular climate of this century.

Now that there is a general idea of the types of presupposi-

tions with which Dr. Schaeffer deals, and the most basic of out-
lines as to how he offers a set of presuppositions for evaluation,
the more specific assumptions about presuppositions which direct and motivate his preevangelistic apologetic must be reviewed. First, Schaeffer asserts that "every person we speak to,
whether shop girl or university student, has a set of presuppositions, whether they have analyzed them or not."[6] So having
a set of presuppositions is not equivalent to consciously maintaining a reflective world view. A set of presuppositions need
necessarily be neither consciously constructed nor unconsciously absorbed; it may be either, or some of both. The point
Schaeffer stresses is that everyone has presuppositions* and
that everyone can be brought to an awareness of them and to
the awareness that they can choose to change them.[7]

A second basic assumption which Schaeffer makes about
presuppositions is that only the presuppositions of historic
Christianity both adequately explain and correspond with the
two environments in which every man must live: the external
world with its form and complexity; and the internal world of
the man's own characteristics as a human being, what Schaeffer
calls "the mannishness of man"—such qualities as a desire for
significance, love, and meaning, and fear of nonbeing, among
others. The strength with which this assumption is made, or the
strength with which this claim is asserted can be seen from two
short quotes: "the solution given in the Bible answers the problem of the universe and man and nothing else does";[8] "it is not
that this is the best answer to existence; it is the only answer."[9]

A somewhat correlative assumption of the pre-evangelistic
approach, and one which Schaeffer presents as giving a definite
direction to the apologist's efforts, is that "no non-Christian can
be consistent with the logic of his presuppositions."[10] In a lecture on apologetics, he has reviewed how he came to such a position of unqualified generalization. Early in his career, Schaeffer maintained that most men are inconsistent in the corre-

*Of course, it must be assumed that Schaeffer's generalization includes all and
only those whose minds are capable of having presuppositions.

spondence of at least some of their daily thoughts and actions with the relevant conclusions which would logically follow from their basic sets of presuppositions. The orientation of his position was that non-Christians would have a difficult time of consistently working out their presuppositions as they lived in the context of their own mannishness and the external world. These two factors, in Schaeffer's view, are in direct and complete correspondence with only the presuppositions of historic Christianity. He held that any non-Christian who was completely consistent with his own presuppositions would maintain each of three positions: he would be "an atheist in religion, an irrationalist in philosophy (including a complete uncertainty concerning natural laws), and completely a-moral in the widest sense."[11] Over the years, Dr. Schaeffer has become convinced that there neither is nor can be such a man. Although he nowhere formally argues that each of these three positions is untenable, some problems attending each are suggested in the four chapters of *He Is There and He Is Not Silent,* certain remarks in his apologetics lecture, and brief passages in his other books.

In fact, these three positions lead us directly into the main thrust of Schaeffer's pre-evangelistic apologetic scheme. That scheme, as has already been mentioned, is to challenge presuppositions alien to the Christian proclamation. I believe that this is carried through by a tripartite argument from design intended to communicate the inadequacies of antithetically non-Christian presuppositions (contradictories to the Christian position), and the truthfulness of basic Christian presuppositional claims.[12]

Before going on I must explain my terminology. I am borrowing the term "argument from design" and using it loosely, not in its traditional, specifically teleological sense. Occasionally, Schaeffer does engage in the traditional teleological argument from design (arguing from the form of the physical universe to the existence of a God who formed it), but this is not what I am referring to by "argument from design." What I mean is any argumentative scheme which

1. looks at and calls attention to the way the universe is, or to the structures of human life within the universe;
2. claims that the "design" (structure) of the universe is such that certain kinds of presuppositions or explanatory hypotheses in fact do explain its being the way it is better than do others;
3. consequently argues the truth of the hypotheses with the greater explanatory power.

Henceforth in this study when I make use of the expression "argument from design" it is to be taken in this general sense unless otherwise specified.

The above mentioned, ultimate non-Christian positions of atheism, irrationality, and amorality correspond to three major areas of human philosophical enquiry traditionally known as metaphysics, epistemology, and ethics, respectively. These are the three divisions or approaches of Schaeffer's argument from design. It must be noted that Dr. Schaeffer himself nowhere identifies his apologetic as an argument from design, and thus never explicitly presents these three areas as clear divisions of such an overall argumentative plan. The book *He Is There and He Is Not Silent* is divided into three major sections of metaphysics, morals, and epistemology. Each is considered as a philosophical problem; but it is never indicated that they are being integrated into an overall inclusive argument from design. In all his books Schaeffer employs the pedagogical techniques of overlap, restatement, and repetition. Because of this, these three areas are treated many times in different contexts.

In the following four chapters I will attempt to bring together, explicate, and interpret the relevant passages concerning each approach of the design argument. Dr. Schaeffer often merely suggests points rather than establishing them by a rigorous line of argument. For that reason I will attempt to support such points by my own arguments when it is helpful for a better understanding of the nature of the argument being undertaken. After Schaeffer's argument from design is presented as clearly as possible in limited space, its usefulness and limitations as an apologetic will be evaluated. The present starting point will be an explication of the metaphysical formulation of his argument, to be followed by the epistemological, and finally the moral.

2

The Metaphysical Argument

ARGUMENT FROM PERSONALITY

REGARDING ATHEISM, Schaeffer argues that such a metaphysical stance fails to adequately account for the existence, form, and complexity of the physical universe and the personality of man. This part of his argument from design is developed in the first chapter of *He Is There and He Is Not Silent*[1] and mentioned more briefly elsewhere.[2] Schaeffer formulates the problem in this way:

> Jean Paul Sartre has said that the basic philosophical question of all questions is this: Why is it that *something* is there rather than *nothing?* He is correct. The great mystery to the materialist is that there is anything there at all.[3]

In his main discussion of this problem, he asserts that basically "there are only three possible answers to this question which would be open to rational consideration."[4] The first possibility is that the present universe came out of absolutely nothing—no matter, energy, motion, personality, or anything. Schaeffer dismisses this option as "unthinkable" because he is unaware of any sustainable argument which might support it.[5]

The second possibility is that "all that now is had an impersonal beginning. This impersonality may be mass, energy, or motion, but they are all impersonal, and all equally impersonal."[6] Hypothesizing a completely impersonal beginning to the universe faces man with the problem of reductionism. If this is the ultimate source of what is, then the universe in its present complexity and man with his "mannishness" are just the results of "the impersonal, plus time, plus chance."[7]   Schaeffer sees this as an insufficient account of what is.

To cast his discussion of the phenomenon of man in *The God Who Is There* into a logical form and extend it somewhat may help to explicate its function as a design argument in relation to the metaphysical question of ultimate and original source-being for the universe. Either human personality is real or it is not real. By "real" I mean that there is something about man in general and the individual man in particular which is qualitatively different from the impersonal, and not merely a function or illusion of the impersonal. An impersonal beginning to the universe would initially seem to render more probable the proposition that personality is not real. However, three problems attend this view which render it difficult if at all possible to maintain.

First, if personality is not real, then what is the status of those characteristics of man which seem to well up from deep within himself? Schaeffer identifies human personality—the "mannishness of man"—with such human desires as the deep-felt needs for meaning, significance, purpose, love, beauty, and order, and the often equally deep-felt abhorrence and fear of non-being. These apparent aspirations would be an enigma if it were held that they are merely advanced systems properties, gradually generated by the survival needs of certain kinds of atomic-molecular-cellular conglomerate groups, and thus are basically homogeneous with all that is nonman in the universe. A plaguing question for such a view concerns the physical genesis of these "properties." What survival value might self-conscious, self-deceiving,* ultimately unfulfillable aspirations have for a physical system? Indeed, the results of many peculiarly human characteristics seem to be self-generically destructive rather than of survival value. In a totally impersonal universe,

---

*Such aspirations are "self-deceiving" because any organism that believes itself to be human and to have a "personality" in a universe without personality is deceived by its own "feelings."

the origin of "apparent personality" characteristics would be inexplicable.

Second, to deny that man is different from all that is nonman is to contradict the testimony that man has borne concerning himself for thousands of years. Schaeffer cites the archeological find of a man buried 30,000 years ago in a grave of flower petals and adds, "Now that's intriguing. You don't find animals burying their dead in flower petals."[8] He also mentions the cave paintings of around 20,000 B.C. as expressing the belief that man is "uniquely distinguished from that which is nonman."[9]

Third, Schaeffer would hold that no man who denies the reality of personality can live consistently with this view. His own aspirations are too powerful to be ignored or denied in practice. An example of such a theory-practice dichotomy can be seen in this passage:

> Many of the same people who say that love is only sexual go through marriage after marriage, hoping to find something more than physical satisfaction. Even when they say love is only sexual, they are looking for something to make 'love' mean what the heart of man longs for it to mean. They simply cannot live consistently with their own view.[10]

These three problems generated by denying the reality of personality—the enigmatic status of human aspirations, the contrary testimony of man throughout history, and the inability to live by such a view—throw us to the other side of the disjunction, to the proposition that personality is real. If human personality is real, then the aspirations of a man are not illusions but are as real and as important as the man is himself as a physical entity, and as he feels them to be. Such a view is consistent with the historical testimony cited, and is also consistent with the way men must live. So the problems attending the claim that personality is an illusion are all left behind.

However, claiming reality for human personality in a foundationally impersonal universe generates three problems of its own. First, if men do indeed have real personalities, real aspirations for personal fulfillment in a universe that is finally impersonal, then those aspirations are ultimately unfulfillable and finally meaningless. Such is Schaeffer's claim.[11] This would make man "the lowest creature on the scale" in a very profound sense, being one whose distinctive nature is contrary to the ground of his being.

The second and more compelling problem, one of derivation and not result, is how personality could ever have arisen from the impersonal. "No one has presented an idea, let alone demonstrated it to be feasible, to explain how the impersonal beginning, plus time, plus chance, can give personality. . . . This is water rising above its source."[12]

The problem is how an impersonal environment could have generated and maintained a form of life whose distinctive nature is both unnecessary for functioning in that environment and finally unfulfillable by that environment. Schaeffer concludes that "only some form of mystical jump will allow us to accept that personality comes from impersonality."[13]

By using the phrase "mystical jump," he is stressing the lack of any deductive necessity, inductive evidence, or process description which would explain the derivation of personality from impersonality. Accepting or positing such a derivation is a nonlogical move—Schaeffer would probably say "an irrational move"—and is not to be accepted when there is a logical alternative. Positing the ultimate nature of the universe to be impersonal is one nonlogical move, and to affirm the reality of human personality, a second nonlogical move is needed. The man who maintains such a view based on two nonlogical moves is faced with a discontinuity between himself and his final environment. However, if a man were to nonlogically posit an ultimately personal nature of reality, his own personality could be seen to flow derivatively from that. There would be one nonlogical move rather than two, and no discontinuity would be involved along the way. A principle of simplicity or parsimony would adjudicate for positing ultimate personality in such a case. Although Schaeffer neither appeals to nor even mentions such a principle, it would seem to be instrumental if not necessary for his rejection of the metaphysical presupposition of ultimate impersonality. By use of the phrase "mystical jump," Schaeffer seems to be faulting the impersonal metaphysic because it contains a nonlogical move. However, that a move is nonlogical cannot be a fault per se to Schaeffer, because it is the nature of Christian as well as non-Christian presuppositions to be nonlogically posited. He seems to be comparing or evaluating presuppositions and their respective results by tacit criteria of simplicity, continuity, or possibly even intellectually satisfying beauty, in the manner of scientific theory evaluation.[14] These criteria are not identified or recognized, but remain unarticulated. Their effect on Schaeffer's apologetic will later be evaluated.

The third problem generated by claiming reality for human personality in a foundationally impersonal universe is one of unity and diversity. Schaeffer makes the claim that an impersonal metaphysic has a problem of unity and diversity, but offers no full explication of this claim, only asserting that such a universe would allow no meaning or significance to diversity.[15] An argument may be formulated involving human personality which clearly shows this problem.

The assertion that human personality is real means that there are particulars or individuals who self-reflectively feel, desire, and claim a significance, meaningfulness, or value for themselves as individuals. However, in a universe in which everything is reducible to a source or content of matter, or energy, or any other impersonal, there is ultimately only unity and homogeneity. This ground of being allows for no special significance to any particular configuration or formation of the basic components, over against any other actual or possible configuration of those components. There is here a contradiction—there is a significant particular in a universe which admits of no significant particulars. An argument attempting to deny the reality of this contradiction could run as follows: The individual's claim to significance in no way brings about the reality of that significance, but is itself clearly false; therefore, there are no significant particulars in the universe and there is no contradiction. It must be replied to this argument that the claim to significance does bring about significance. As the individual is able to be self-cognizant as well as other-cognizant, his very self-cognizance renders him individually significant over against any other individual. This is not to say that self-cognizance fulfills the total individual felt need for significance, but only that it does itself create a significance of the individual. So, claiming the reality of human personality in a foundationally impersonal universe seems to be a contradiction. There is here no evident reconciliation of unity and diversity. If there is real significance to the unity of an homogeneous impersonality, then there can be no significant diversity of particulars. If there is real significance to the diversity of particulars, then there can be no significant unity of homogeneous impersonality.†

On the basis of the preceding discussion it would seem that, given an impersonal beginning to what is, we cannot maintain either that human personality is real or that it is not real, without serious problems. By the logical law of excluded middle we must, of course, choose either real or unreal as the status of personality. The choice of "real" answered the problems generated by "unreal," but not vice versa. Therefore, we seem to be on the right track in claiming reality for human personality. Since a basically impersonal universe would raise problems for such a claim, we are ready to consider the third metaphysical alternative offered by Schaeffer: that the ultimate origin and ground of being for the universe is personal.

If the beginning or final nature of the universe is personal, then the three problems which attended the claim of reality for human personality in an impersonal universe disappear. There is no longer a problem of the impossibility of ultimate fulfillment for the aspirations of human personality in such a uni-

---

†By "significance" is meant simply importance or individual consequence. An individual item is significant if its particular individuality has an import. After formulating this argument, I found a striking parallel in Reinhold Niebuhr, *The Nature and Destiny of Man* (New York: Scribner, 1949), 1:55.

verse. The person surrounded by final impersonality would be estranged as an isolated anomaly, denied fulfillment as personal existent, and destined also to ultimate alienation, likely to culminate in extinction within the original consuming envelope of the impersonal—finally seen to be the antipersonal. However, if the ultimate environment of the universe were personal, it would be clear that human personality would not be qualitatively alien to that, its final environment. In fact, this affinity would be a kind of affirmation to the individual that the congruence of his own being with the very ground of all being in itself entails the possibility of fulfillment.

Second, in a basically personal universe there would be no problem of origin or derivation of human personality. As mentioned before, there would be no discontinuity between the final environment and man. Human personality would be consistent with the intrinsic nature of the ground of its being. The origin of human personality would be rooted in the ultimate personality and would thereby be explicable.

Third, the contradiction of unity and diversity present in a finally impersonal universe containing real human personality is absent from a finally personal universe. The universal principle of unity in such a universe, rather than being a homogeneity of basic impersonality, is a common source or rootedness in, dependence upon, and relation to the ultimate personal ground of being. This significant unity can exist simultaneously with a significant diversity of personal individuals, as they are individually derived from, and as meaningful entities individually reflect, the nature of the ultimate personality.

On the basis of the foregoing discussion, an ultimately personal metaphysic alone seems adequate to logically subsume the phenomena of human personality. The line of reasoning presented has followed the form of a theistic argument from design, and it is important to note that nothing other than the characteristic of ultimate personality has been specified concerning the *theos* (Greek for "God," the intended conclusion of any theistic argument). This lack of further specification is due

to an inherent limitation of arguments from design. All that
has been concluded is that a personal beginning and ultimate
ground of being is needed for a universe containing human personality. The question is still unanswered as to what specific
kind of personality began, and is foundational to, the universe.
There are innumerable types or varieties of personal beginning
which could be postulated to meet this need. Design arguments
based on the phenomena of human personality or mental experience can cogently contend for theism (ultimate personality)
as against naturalism (ultimate impersonality), but cannot adjudicate between rival theistic positions. For example, Juda-
ism, Islam, polytheism, or practically any other theistic religion could employ an argument such as the foregoing as evidence against atheism or naturalism.

It is at this point that I must reveal what I have done in the
argument thus far, and for what reasons. Dr. Schaeffer has suggested the three problems attending personality in an impersonal universe, although none are fully argued by him. In fact,
the substance of each of the first two is merely adumbrated,
whereas the third—unity and diversity—is hardly more than
given a name. Consequently, I have tried to accurately fill out
the first two, but must assume practically full responsibility
for the presentation of the third, as it is only my attempt to render understandable and logical a problem left greatly undefined by Schaeffer himself. However, all three answers given
to these problems are completely my own. I have presumed to
formulate and present my own answers to problems raised by
Dr. Schaeffer in preparation for his own answers to demonstrate
what I believe to be the only valid direction this argument from
design can take. Dr. Schaeffer desires to put forth the metaphysical presuppositions of an orthodox Christian faith as better in explanatory power than any other set of presuppositions
available to or held by modern men. In fact, his claim extends
even further, to the assertion that the Christian presuppositions
are the *only* ones which answer the problems facing man. In
order to support this claim, he formulates an argument from

design. Thus, he tries to make this argument reach all the way from its basic data to his specific conclusions: the orthodox Christian presuppositions. Since such conclusions are beyond the valid extensions of a design argument, Schaeffer fails to complete the argument in its own valid form (with the final conclusion of merely a personal beginning yielding answers such as my own three) and proceeds to offer two additional principles or criteria by which to define the personal beginning into the specific presuppositions which he offers. He asserts that "once we consider a personal beginning, we have yet another choice to make. This is the next step: are we going to choose the answer of God or gods?"[16]

To answer this question, the two criteria are presented. First, the ultimate personality must be "big enough."‡[17] The ancient Greek gods are cited as too limited in their finite personality to provide an adequate point of reference for absolutes which could extend over the whole of reality. Here Schaeffer states that "only a personal-infinite God is big enough."[18] The notion of infinitude as it is here used is not explicated by Schaeffer. There is no argument offered as to why a God infinitely extensive in space, time, or any other mode is necessary for "absolutes" (which is also a term undefined by him). In one passage, a very brief argument is offered to show that personality and infinitude are not incompatible:

> Modern man has driven a wedge between the personal and the infinite and says that personality equals finiteness. He has equated personality with limitedness. But the Christian says that the only limitation which personality intrinsically must have is that it cannot be impersonal at the same time.[19]

However, granted that personality and infinitude are not incompatible, an argument for the possibility of a personal-infinite God in no way establishes the necessity for or actuality of such a God, which clearly seems to be the intention of Schaeffer's first criterion. Therefore, this conclusion of Schaef-

---

‡The question must be asked, Big enough for what? It is not clear what he is requiring.

fer's stands as a specification unwarranted by any argument offered by him, although it is presented with the finality of a tightly reasoned conclusion.

The second criterion presented by Schaeffer for specifying
the kind of personal beginning to be postulated is that it should
provide or consist of an ultimate personal unity and diversity.[20]
He often mentions that every philosophy must struggle with the
problem of unity and diversity; but, again, he himself never ex-
plicates the nature of the problem. On the basis of this second
criterion—the need for a significant unity and a significant diversity in the ultimate personal ground of being for the universe—Schaeffer puts forth the orthodox Christian concept of
the Trinity, one God in three persons.[21] The Trinity is postulated as "an answer for unity and diversity,"[22] although the
precise manner in which it provides an answer is left unexplained. Once again, the popular and suggestive nature of Dr.
Schaeffer's books must be remembered. He quite often merely
alludes to a philosophical problem and suggests the adequacy
of the orthodox Christian presuppositions to provide an answer.
Thus, details are left unmentioned, and many arguments un-
stated. However mysterious a personal diversity within the final
unity of the ultimate personal ground of being might be, many
if not most readers will intuit that the significant applicability
of this paradoxical pair of substantives to the divine Being
somehow presents a solution or guaranteed resolution to whatever problems attend them on lesser levels. Although the Trinity may be found to answer problems of unity and diversity, this
second criterion in no way necessitates a trinitarian postula-
tion. Thus again as with the first criterion, no argument has
established this specification offered by Dr. Schaeffer. If these
two specifications—a personal-infinite God, three persons in
One, a Trinity—are derived from another source, then Schaeffer's two criteria can at most move toward showing that they
are indeed possible and productive specifications of the personal beginning of the universe. They have not been logically
extended from the design argument as necessary specifications

of its conclusion, but have been brought in from elsewhere as functional postulates. The problem here is that Dr. Schaeffer has not identified their source, biblical revelation, but has presented them as if they were tightly argued conclusions, universally acceptable. It would not be a weakening of the orthodox position to admit that certain doctrines or specifications about the nature or being of God are derived from revelation; rather, such an admission would help to clarify both the status of the Christian claims, and the nature and source of human knowledge and argument concerning God.

A somewhat compelling argument from design and two slightly enigmatic criteria have gotten us to this point. A summary is here in order. Dr. Schaeffer is attempting to challenge the presuppositions of modern men which are alien to the Christian Gospel and at the same time to substantiate those of the orthodox faith. By stressing the importance of human personality, he has entered a fruitful argumentative direction, one in which theism is forcefully presentable. The foregoing discussion has concluded the "apparent necessity" of a personal beginning—theism—and has moved toward showing the possibility of orthodox Christian trinitarian theism.

I have used the phrase "apparent necessity" both to preserve and to qualify Schaeffer's vocabulary. Preserving it yields insight into his attitudes toward the argument, qualifying it yields insight into the relation between that attitude and the logical status of the argument itself. The conclusion of theism which has been reached is not "necessary" in any deductively logical sense. At most it is highly probable as compared with atheism or naturalism. Thus the word "necessity," in distinction from what often seems to be Schaeffer's intention, cannot be used here in its logical denotation but only as it connotes the strength of the argument's adequacy, psychologically received (hence the qualifier "apparent"). I say that Dr. Schaeffer has only *moved toward* showing the possibility of orthodox Christian trinitarian theism because *showing* that possibility would involve answering questions which he does not consider.

For example, some antagonists or skeptics have pointed to the philosophically debated "problem of evil" as a proof that the orthodox Christian conception of God is logically incoherent and therefore logically impossible. Others impugn language about God, questioning whether human languages are adequate even for considering the possibility or impossibility of there being a God as Christians proclaim.

Of course, Christian philosophers have presented many avenues of approach to answering these questions, some of which yield very effective results in defense of the logical possibility and linguistic discussability of the Christian concept of God. However, as none of these answers is explicitly affirmed or employed by Dr. Schaeffer in his published arguments, it cannot be said that *he* has shown the possibility of the orthodox Christian position; only that he has moved toward that conclusion. I must add that, with the right arguments, he easily could have attained the conclusion that Christian theism is possible. Dr. Schaeffer's oversights weaken only his argumentative conclusions, not the orthodox Christian claims. A necessary conclusion of an argument based on actual data will itself be actual; however, a possible or even highly probable conclusion of an argument based on actual data will itself not necessarily be actual. There is a logical gap of uncertainty between the possible or probable and the actual. The significance and implications of this gap in Schaeffer's presentation will be considered later on in this study.

ARGUMENT FROM ORDER

It will be remembered that we are analyzing the pre-evangelistic, presuppositional apologetic strategy of Dr. Schaeffer as presented in the three areas of metaphysics, epistemology, and ethics. In the area of metaphysics, the argument from design formulated by Schaeffer is motivated from two directions: from a consideration of the phenomena of human personality, and from a consideration of the form and complexity of the physical universe. The former has been analyzed, the latter hardly mentioned to this point. I will present only a brief discussion of the argument that he offers from form and complexity, as I believe that it is less conclusive than that from personality, and hence is less supportive of his specific claims.

Concerning the form or order of the universe, Schaeffer states that:

> the universe has order. It is not a chaos. One is able to pro-
> ceed from the particulars of being to some understanding of
> its unity. One is able to move ever deeper into the universe
> and yet never come upon a precipice of incoherence.[23]

Anticipating that Schaeffer is likely to argue from order to an Orderer, an antagonist might at this point already wish to raise an objection. In *Novum Organum*, Francis Bacon declared that "the human understanding is of its own nature prone to suppose the existence of more order and regularity in the world than it finds."[24] So it might be objected that much or most, if not all of the order to which Schaeffer points is only apparent or supposed rather than real.

The contention that "all is finally chaotic, irrational, and absurd," a view "expressed with great finesse in the existential world of thinking and in the theater of the absurd," leads to the assertion that to ultimate problems in the area of metaphysics (as in all other areas) "there is no logical, rational answer."[25] Schaeffer argues that this view cannot be held in practice. The man who avers that there is no real ordered form to the universe must still leave the room via a door or window, and by his very inability to walk through the solid walls refutes his own claim.[26] That such a man can even make an intelligible claim renders the assertion of that specific claim null; for if there were no real order at all, "All discussion would come to an end. Communication would end. We would have only a series of meaningless sounds—blah, blah, blah."[27]

Even the theater of the absurd fails to follow this claim in practice, for "it is always trying to communicate its view that

one cannot communicate."[28] Thus, a position that the universe
is totally disorderly or chaotic is not consistently maintainable.

As soon as some order is admitted, Schaeffer maintains that
a metaphysical discussion must consider the two rational answers to the beginning of the universe and its present ordered
form: either the beginning was impersonal or it was personal.
Concerning the former possibility he asserts that "beginning
with the impersonal there is no explanation for the complexity
of the universe. . . ."[29] Here, the order of the universe is said to
be not simple but complex. Elsewhere, the following is offered
as support:

> For several years Murray Eden at MIT has been using high
> speed computers to calculate the possibility of whether on the
> basis of chance there could be so much complexity in the uni-
> verse within any acceptable amount of time. His conclusion
> is that the possibility is zero.[30]

No other arguments are presented to validate a move from the
data of order and complexity through the rejection of an impersonal beginning as inadequate to the conclusion of a personal beginning or, further, to the orthodox Christian identifi-
cation of God. Since David Hume's *Dialogues Concerning Natural Religion,* the problems attending this kind of argumentative direction have been clear.[31] I will not reiterate them here
but will instead refer the interested reader to an article written
by R. G. Swinburne in the journal *Philosophy* (1968), where
reformulation of the argument from order is given convincingly
and the objections of Hume are considered individually. However, in general it is agreed that the ambiguity of the data render this form of design argument much more problematic than
that beginning with personality.

Dr. Schaeffer claimed that the completely consistent non-
Christian would be "an atheist in religion, an irrationalist in
philosophy (including a complete uncertainty concerning natural laws), and completely a-moral in the widest sense."[32] The
metaphysical formulation of the design argument seems to be

directed toward pointing out the problems generated by atheism, which is equated with the view of an impersonal beginning to the universe. I believe that he has successfully raised serious problems for such a position. However, the force with which he presents the orthodox Christian presupposition of a personal-infinite triune God as exclusively adequate in providing "the only answer to the metaphysical problem of existence"[33] is clearly unwarranted by his arguments. He has moved in the direction of showing it to be a possible answer, not "the only answer."

3

The Epistemological Argument:
The Problem

ANOTHER KIND of design argument, operating from epistemological considerations, seems directed toward demonstrating the problems attending the second alleged position of a consistent non-Christian—irrationalism in philosophy. Once again, an argument from design is not presented as such, but I believe that this schema renders understandable the intent of many disjoined passages and discussions referring or alluding to epistemological concerns. Basic to the problems to be put forth by Schaeffer is an understanding of his discussion of the presuppositional shift of modern science. Modern science began, he said, from the presuppositions that the universe was created by a reasonable God in a reasonable form, and that man could, by use of his reason, discover that form. Physically, the universe offered to the scientist a "uniformity of natural causes" in a limited or open system. Both God and man were free from the complete physical determinism of a closed "machine." God stood as epistemological Guarantor for man. However, in the eighteenth, and primarily the nineteenth, century, God was excluded from the machine, and man was included in it: the uniformity of natural causes in a *closed* system.[1]

Schaeffer sees this development as posing a real problem of how a man can know that he really knows what he thinks he knows.[2] He cites positivism as the major attempt of modern men maintaining the closed system presupposition to establish an epistemological certitude, and offers three general criticisms in rejection of it. First, he mentions Michael Polanyi's book *Personal Knowledge* and says:

> Polanyi argues that positivism is inadequate because it does not consider the knower of what is known. It acts as if the knower may be overlooked and yet have full knowledge of certain things, as though the knower knew without actually being there. Or you might say positivism does not take into account the knower's theories or presuppositions.[3]

Second, Schaeffer claims that the system of positivism itself cannot provide for its own first move:

> You simply begin nakedly with nothing there. You have no reason within the system to know that the data is data, or that what is reaching you is data.[4]

Schaeffer means by this that positivism cannot guarantee that there is any difference in its first move between "reality and fantasy."

Third, he asserts that positivism offers no guarantee that there is a correlation between the thought of the observer and the thing observed. There are many possible ways of developing this criticism, which is left undeveloped by Schaeffer. In evaluating the accuracy of a man's conclusions concerning the physical world it is necessary to examine his capacity for accurately receiving data from external sources through his senses, and the validity of his reasoning processes which induce and infer from that data. Concerning the reliability of the senses, Michel de Montaigne argued in the sixteenth century that "all knowledge comes through our senses, and the senses are, as experience shows, completely unreliable."[5] "Now since our state accommodates things to itself and transforms them according to itself, we do not know what things are in truth, for nothing comes to us except falsified and altered by our senses."[6]

This skepticism of the senses, derived from the Pyrrhonians in Montaigne's formulation, is still a real problem for men who hold the presuppositions of a closed universe.

In his book *Miracles: A Preliminary Study,* C. S. Lewis

offers a persuasive argument that in a naturalistic universe (Schaeffer's "closed system"), there would be no validity for human thought. In a physical system in which no event occurs without a prior physical cause and every event is ultimately dependent on every other event, there can be no completely original event. Any collocation of atoms occurs only because it was determined to occur, whether by lawful or random ordering of prior conditions. In such a universe, every human thought that occurs is merely the result of "brute force" (the forced patterning of the brain's atoms), which as a cause is classed as "irrational" rather than "rational." There is no guarantee or even reason to believe that any given thought will truly correspond to a reality outside of the thinker.[7]

An antagonist who believed the universe to be in fact "naturalistic" or ultimately an impersonal closed system could reply to Lewis' argument that, if this conclusion validly follows from the way the universe indeed is (naturalistic in the eyes of the antagonist), then there is no guarantee or even reason to believe that this conclusion, being a thought, truly corresponds to any reality outside Lewis' mind ("the thinker"). Consequently, Lewis' argument itself would not have to be accepted as true. However, it could be answered that the basic premise of the antagonist's reply, that the universe is naturalistic, could itself not be asserted as true about the universe (because of the reasons offered by Lewis) and that, consequently, this reply could never be formulated as a true statement.

The presupposition of the uniformity of natural causes in a closed system seems to involve serious epistemological difficulties, as the brief development of Schaeffer's critique of positivism has shown. The closed system has brought with it another problem, which he sees as the most serious and pervasive of our century. In fact, he has repeatedly and emphatically identified this phenomenon as the distinctive mark of the twentieth century intellectual and cultural climate. In Schaeffer's view, the problem is that the attainment of knowledge in the areas of human significance, meaning, and personal hope has been methodologically separated from the attainment of knowledge in every other area, creating what he calls "a divided field of knowledge."[8]

Dr. Schaeffer's first two books, *The God Who Is There* and *Escape from Reason,* as suggestive essays of intellectual history, trace the history of this division to roots in the thought of Thomas Aquinas. According to Schaeffer, "from the time of the Greeks onward," the schools of philosophy in the West shared three important principles in common. First, they were rationalistic. By this he means that they held that "man begins absolutely and totally from himself, gathers the information concerning the particulars and formulates the universals."[9]

Thus, the use of "rationalism" here seems to be that of human epistemological autonomy. In a glossary, he defines rationalism as "any philosophy or system of thought that begins with man alone, in order to try to find a unified meaning to life."[10]

Rationalism could be further specified along these lines as a philosophical orientation which does not recognize the epistemological primacy, or even the validity, of an alleged divine revelation to man.

Second, "they all believed in the rational." To explicate this principle, Schaeffer remarks in two points that "they acted upon the basis that man's aspiration for the validity of reason was well founded," and that "they thought in terms of antithesis. If a certain thing was true, the opposite was not true."[11]

The terms rational, rationality, and reason are nowhere clearly defined by Dr. Schaeffer. They are used by him as apparently very important, meaningful and specific denotations, often serving to clinch an argument or empower a criticism, but their meanings are only connotatively available to the reader, ascertainable only as somehow related to classical logic (as in the above-mentioned example of antithesis, or the law of non-contradiction). Further on in this study, the concept of rationality or reason motivating and directing Schaeffer's apologetic will be examined, but here it is only necessary to note that the notions of rationality and irrationality will be important in the historical presentation of the epistemological division or divided field of knowledge.

The third principle common to the schools of philosophy in the West was, according to Schaeffer, the hope that a unified field of knowledge might be constructed. There was a hope that "by means of rationalism plus rationality," men would be able to find "a complete answer," "an answer that would encompass all of thought and all of life." Schaeffer insists that this was to be done with the singular logical methodology of antithesis.[12]

"But at a certain point the attempt to spin out a unified optimistic humanism ceased. . . . In the end the philosophers came to the realization that they could not find this unified rationalistic circle, and so, departing from the classical methodology of antithesis, they shifted the concept of truth and modern man was born."[13]

Before explicating this claim, we must turn our discussion to Thomas Aquinas and briefly recount the historical argument presented by Schaeffer which culminates in this "birth" of modern man. That argument follows.

Dr. Schaeffer points to the anthropology of Aquinas as significant in the epistemological developments of the West leading to modern man. His contention is that, for Aquinas "the will of man was fallen but the intellect was not."[14] This position promoted an autonomy of the intellect to engage in natural theology and philosophical reasoning apart from the grace of God and His revelation in the Scriptures.* Thus, in theologically dominated Europe, a dichotomy arose between "nature and grace," which Schaeffer diagrams (see p. 45).†[15]

Following this very brief exposition of Aquinas, Schaeffer traces what he sees as the increasing importance of nature in the arts as well as in theology resulting from his thought. He further

---

*The philosophical position of Siger of Brabant is an example of this.

†The accuracy of this diagram could be questioned; e.g., should God the Creator not be below the line and the Trinity above the line?

GRACE, THE HIGHER: God the creator; heaven and heavenly things; the unseen and its influence on the earth; man's soul; unity

---

NATURE, THE LOWER: The created; earth and earthly things; the visible and what nature and man do on the earth; man's body; diversity

claims that, with the human intellect operating autonomously in the area of nature, a process began which he terms "nature eating up grace," the natural overwhelming the heavenly. This process is presented as mirrored in representative paintings of the fifteenth century in which the Madonna, previously iconographical in depiction, began to be painted in the likeness of well-known mistresses.[16] The process is also illustrated by his accounts of the rise and development of modern science and its progression from a metaphysically Christian view of the universe to a position in which the physical universe was a closed system—God pushed out and man trapped in.

Schaeffer claims that the conception of the universe as an all-inclusive machine began to dominate thought with the Newtonians.[17] He then cites the next important thinker of this progression: "Jean-Jacques Rousseau is crucial at this point, because he changed the formulation from 'nature and grace' to 'nature and freedom,' absolute freedom."[18] Schaeffer claims that as Rousseau and the men around him were faced with the machine which was trapping them, they reacted against absorption by science and held out autonomous individual freedom as an ideal. He attributes to them a struggle to avoid being trapped by either nature or society as the machine.[19] "At this time we find that nature is now really so totally autonomous that determinism begins to emerge."[20]

Human freedom is not logically compatible with a universe

that is totally deterministic. Thus, freedom is posited in logical tension with nature, and rationality is strained.

The other figure that Schaeffer cites at this point is Kant. It would seem that Kant would be a very important participant in the development of the divided field of knowledge, but Schaeffer does little more than mention his name in each of his historical discussions. However, he does claim that Kant was not able to bring the noumenal and phenomenal worlds together; hence arises the same kind of dichotomy between the physical particulars of the universe and that which gives meaning.

Here is a unifying factor that Schaeffer never explicitly mentions but which I believe to be the glue that can bring together his discussion thus far in preparation for what follows. Allow me to repeat it for emphasis. The various dichotomies found in Aquinas, Rousseau, and Kant really represent only one dichotomy, although couched in different terms: a dichotomy between the physical particulars of the universe wherein there is no special significance or meaning for man who is just one among other physical entities, and a nonphysical realm of existence of experience wherein significance, meaning, and values can be found for man.

With this in mind we come to G. W. F. Hegel, in many ways the focal point of Schaeffer's historical survey. It was with Hegel that the classical methodology of antithesis was superseded by the new dialectical methodology of synthesis. For Hegel, synthesis was to be a logical move—the thesis and its antithesis would generate a certain, necessary, predictable synthesis. Although the concept of logic or reasoning underwent a change, the new logic was seen as an applicable and sufficient cognitive methodology for approaching questions in all areas of life, whether of mechanics or of meaning, as had been the old. However, Hegel's departure from mere antithesis and presentation of the triadic, synthetic movement is referred to by Schaeffer as "the door into the line of despair."[21] The "line of despair" is one of Schaeffer's distinctive concepts which refers to a general date line around a half century to a century after the time of Hegel (d.1831). During this period of time, according to Schaeffer, rationalistic philosophers in general "despaired" of ever finding a unified answer to life on the basis of classical, antithetical rationality or reasoning.

Soren Kierkegaard is identified by Schaeffer as the first significant thinker who "went below the line."[22]

> What proposition did he add to Hegel's thought that made the difference? Kierkegaard came to the conclusion that you could not arrive at synthesis by reason. Instead, you achieved everything of real importance by a leap of faith. So he separated absolutely the rational and logical from faith.[23]

So Schaeffer claims that Kierkegaard was the man who divided "the field of knowledge" completely, methodologically separating questions of human significance, meaning, and value from the grasp of logic. He diagrams:[24]

FAITH

The rational and the logical

Elsewhere he continues, "After Kierkegaard, rationality is seen as leading to pessimism . . . any kind of optimism one could have concerning meaning would have to be in the area of the non-rational. . . ."[25]

This is the dichotomy or division of knowledge: the physical or mechanical aspects of life are dealt with by rational, logical thought; but all questions of significance, meaning, and value must be finally answered by a nonrational move, some kind of faith "leap." The basic type of dichotomy found in Aquinas, Rousseau, and Kant, whose halves had been previously held together, however much in tension, now "sprang apart"[26] in an absolute division.

In summarizing the place of Kierkegaard and that which

followed him in dividing the field of knowledge, Schaeffer states: ‡[27]

> The important thing about him is that, when he put forth the concept of a leap of faith, he became in a real way the father of all modern existential thought, both secular and theological.
>
> As a result of this, from that time on, if rationalistic man wants to deal with the real things of human life (such as purpose, significance, the validity of love) he must discard rational thought about them and make a gigantic, non-rational leap of faith. The rationalistic framework had failed to produce an answer on the basis of reason, and so all hope of a uniform field of knowledge had to be abandoned. We get the resulting dichotomy like this:

The Non-rational and Non-logical	Existential experience; the final experience; the first order experience.
The Rational and Logical	Only particulars, no purpose, no meaning. Man is a machine.

In *The God Who Is There* and *Escape from Reason,* Dr. Schaeffer traces this dichotomy and identifies the nonrational leap as manifested in three main "schools" of secular existential thought, the drug culture, modern art, music, general culture (literature, drama, cinema, and other mass media), and theology. There is no need to recapitulate those discussions here. Let it suffice to say that the dichotomy is seen by Schaeffer to be present in every facet of twentieth-century life and culture. It will be remembered that this dichotomy is not only seen by Schaeffer to be pervasive, but also to be an epistemological problem, and further, a serious one. Since he himself mostly either adumbrates or implies the epistemological difficulties attending a nonlogical movement toward meaning, I will attempt to define three problems culled generally from his discussions, and further develop them.

---

‡The upper half of the diagram, in its many various forms presented by Schaeffer, is called by him "the upper storey," or "upstairs"; the lower half, "the lower storey," or "downstairs."

In regard to a nonlogical search for meaning through experience, Schaeffer refers to followers of Karl Jaspers and their orientation toward and dependence on the "final experience":

> People who follow Jaspers have come to me and said "I have had a final experience". They never expect me to ask them what it was . . .
>
> The fact that it is an *existential* experience means that it cannot be communicated. It is not possible to communicate content with regard to the experience which they have had.[28]

The noncommunicability of the existential experience creates two great problems. One is the isolation of the individual man from others. When the source of a man's own personal meaning is unsharable, not even communicable, a terrible isolation results. "How do we have any categories to enable us to move into the other person's thought world? This is the modern man's alienation; this is the blackness which so many modern people face, the feeling of being totally alienated."[29]

Such alienation is forcefully expressed in much of modern art. In reference to some of Alberto Giacometti's sculptures, Raoul-Jean Moulin has commented that "the squares are areas limited by a base, where people pass each other with a long, even stride, strangers to each other, accustomed to their own loneliness, imprisoned in their own situation."[30]

This isolation, alienation, and mutually exclusive imprisonment of men estranged from each other in that which alone gives meaning and significance to their individual persons, creates the horrible problem of the unknowability of others.

Along with the problem of knowing others is the problem of knowing with others. When the source of personal significance, meaning, and value is a nonrational, noncommunicable experience, there is neither an intersubjective basis for common knowledge nor an intersubjective direction for common action in regard to collective human problems. John Macquarrie has commented:

> But so many of the most pressing problems of the contempo-

rary world concern the relations between groups or corporate
entities—national and international bodies, corporations,
races, trade unions and the like . . . we need some positive
guidance in these areas and it is doubtful if existentialism has
much to offer. In spite of their genuine insistence that all existence is inescapably a being-with-others, most existentialist
philosophies take the existence of the individual as the start-
ing-point, and when this first step has been taken, perhaps the
bias toward the existence of the single individual makes itself
felt in all the subsequent analyses.[31]

Existential experience as the only source of meaning is scan-
dalously particular rather than universal in scope, entailing
problems of both knowing others and knowing with others.

The other problem generated by holding experience, or especially the "final experience," as sole locus of meaning is expressed by Schaeffer:

> Try to put yourself for a moment in such a man's place. He
> has a deep problem, for he hangs everything to do with his
> certainty of being and the hope of significance upon some
> titanic experience he had at a specific point in the past . . .
> Nor can the individual verbalize to himself what has hap-
> pened. Tomorrow morning they may say, "Yesterday I had
> an experience". The day after they still say, "I had an experi-
> ence". A month and a year later they are hanging on grimly
> to their only hope of significance and certainty of being by re-
> peating, "I know I had an experience". The horror of this
> situation is due to their putting their hope on a non-rational,
> non-logical, non-communicable experience.[32]

In addition to being isolated from others, the individual is isolated from his own source of meaning which vanishes into a
nonrepeatable past—the final loneliness.

In regard to a nonlogical search for meaning through action,
Schaeffer comments on Jean Paul Sartre:

> He says that we live in an absurd universe. The total, he says,
> is ridiculous. Nevertheless you try to authenticate yourself

by an act of the will. It does not really matter in which direction you act as long as you act.[33]

John Macquarrie elaborates further, specifying the problem
of a move in this direction:

> The warning is that when men do begin to let reason slip, to
> claim that intensity and passion are above rational criticism,
> and to prize the absurd and paradoxical, a terrible danger
> looms on the horizon. It is the danger not just of the irra-
> tional but of the anti-rational, and the anti-rational can as
> easily assume the forms of inhuman cruelty as of quixotic gen-
> erosity.[34]

If the source of personal significance, meaning, and value for
an individual is to be nonlogically resident in or generated by
his own personal choices to action, or even if it is to be actively
posited by him nonlogically, then there are no "reasonable"
controls on what the interpretation of the meaning involved
with the action might be. In such a case, the meaning referent
of a man's life may shift and change in an indeterminate flux,
plaguing him with recurrent uncertainty concerning his precise
orientation in the cosmos; or it may be arbitrarily fixed by him
who, as the arbiter, is vulnerable to the attack of self-doubt,
which here entails a profound epistemological uncertainty concerning the status of the determined referential locus of his own
personal significance, meaning and value.

In addition to the problems of isolation attending a nonlogical search for meaning through experience and the disjunctive
problem of indeterminacy or arbitrary determinacy attending
a search through action, there is a third general problem generated by a dichotomized epistemology, potentially troubling
to any kind of nonlogical attempt to deal with questions of human meaning. This is the problem of distinguishing between
reality and fantasy. This problem has actually been seen before
in Schaeffer's three criticisms of positivism. He specifies it further:

At the very heart of the thing is the loss of distinction between reality and fantasy by the taking of drugs. But even if modern man does not take drugs, he has no categories once he has moved out of the lower area of reason. Downstairs he is already dead; he is only a machine, and none of these things have [sic] any meaning. But as soon as he moves upstairs into the area of the upper-storey mysticism, all that is left is a place with no categories to distinguish the inner world from the outer world with any certainty or to distinguish what is in his head from that which is in the external world.

What we are left with today is the fact that modern man has no categories to enable him to be at all sure of the difference between what is real and what is only in his head. Many who come to us at L'Abri have suffered this loss of distinction between reality and fantasy.[35]

Schaeffer's claim is that the man who, dealing with the important questions of human existence, achieves his own personal answers and hope nonrationally or nonlogically, is isolated on the deepest personal level from the universe around him. Once logical and evidential reasoning has been abandoned in one area, with nonlogical moves being an accepted methodology, there is no universally guiding principle whereby the individual may know when or when not to appropriate logical conclusions rather than merely personal conclusions. Neither is there any intersubjective standard by which to determine whether any particular conclusion is better (i.e., more warranted or accurate) than any other in those areas where evidence and logic are put aside.

One criticism must be brought forth here concerning Schaeffer's presentation of this problem. It is clear that distinguishing between reality and fantasy may be a serious problem for anyone who achieves his answers in the area of human meaning by nonlogical moves. However, as was mentioned earlier in this study, it is also clear that no world view, and in fact no human knowledge at all, is without dependence on the nonlogical or personal contributions of the knower. This is true of the orthodox Christian presuppositions and world view as well as of any other. Therefore, the fact that there are nonlogical moves in a reasoning process cannot per se be criticized as a weakness of that process. However, this often seems to be what Dr. Schaeffer is doing. He does not fully acknowledge the nonlogical contributions of every human knower to his own knowledge, in whatever area. If the mere presence of nonlogical moves in a reasoning process generates a problem of reality and fantasy, then this problem is inescapable, present in every epistemology, and therefore a damaging criticism of no particular epistemology.

However, this acknowledgment does not vitiate the thrust of Schaeffer's argument. It is not, or should not be, the mere presence of nonlogical moves in a reasoning process which is the real object of his criticism. Suppose there are two propositions, A and B. Suppose also that A is already maintained as true and itself offers great inductive evidence that B is true. No matter how great the amount of inductive evidence for B, B cannot be appropriated or known as true without a personal, nonlogical move of the knower.§ However, once B *is* held as true, it can be seen to be compatible with all that is known about A, and is not itself isolated from or contrary to the evidence of A. Remembering the necessarily personal coefficients of logic, it can be said that B is a logical conclusion of A, or that the question of B was dealt with logically from the perspective of A. Now, again, Dr. Schaeffer does not himself acknowledge in any of his writings that this is the nature of logical thought or reasoning. He nowhere mentions the personal, nonlogical aspects of rational thought. In fact, the tendency of his writings is to give the impression that logical reasoning is a totally dispassionate, disinterested, nonpersonal, mechanical operation, as has been mentioned earlier in this study.

Schaeffer has claimed that for modern men who presuppose that the universe is a closed system (a naturalistic universe),

§This can also be argued for deductive conclusions, but the personal contributions are not at first as obvious.

the physical or mechanical aspects of life are dealt with logically, but that in questions of significance, meaning, and value for the individual man, the physical environment viewed as a closed system plus logical reasoning yields only pessimism concerning the nature and hope of man (man being homogenous with nonman, or unfulfillable). Thus he claims, men have departed from logic in these questions and have leapt into a nonlogical, nonrational, "upper storey" realm with the hope of thereby finding meaning. It is this movement that draws his criticism. It is not the kind of nonlogical move in the above example of A and B which draws his criticism (else all thought would be criticized—a self-contradiction), but a very different kind of move.

Suppose A represents the conjunction of all known propositions concerning the physical universe, viewed as a closed system. The direction of Schaeffer's argument is that, on the basis of A, the logical answer to questions of man's unique significance and hope (or the possibility of fulfillment for the aspirations of the mannishness of man) would be B, a conclusion of reductionism, ultimate unfulfillability, and pessimism. However, he claims that modern men have not been able to live with a conclusion such as B and have nonlogically posited some form of a -B ("not B" or "non B") conclusion.|| There of course would be nonlogical, personal moves involved in the process of concluding or accepting B. But, as was shown in the previous example, B, once held, would be evidentially compatible with A and would not be isolated from or contrary to that evidence of A. However, -B, the kind of move or conclusion being criticized by Schaeffer, once held, is not evidentially compatible with, is completely isolated from, and is contrary to that evidence of A. So B and -B have been reached by different types of nonlogical movement. With B, nonlogical steps have been taken in the direction of the evidence; with -B a nonlogical leap has been made in an opposite direction from that of the

||Both B and -B can be considered ranges or sets of propositions; for example, B can include such variants as B_1, B_2, etc. (the same holding true for -B).

evidence. With B there is a unified field of knowledge; with -B there is a dichotomy, -B being inconsistent with A and concluded by a different methodology than that by which the propositions of A are related and the conclusion B is reached.

In this kind of dichotomy, Schaeffer sees the acute problem of distinguishing reality and fantasy. The infinitely many possible variations or specifications of the -B conclusion are all methodologically and thus evidentially disassociated from all else that is claimed as known by the knower. There are therefore, as he has pointed out, no categories for making that important distinction in this vital area of personal knowledge.

4

The Epistemological Argument:
The Answer

IN HIS GENERAL CRITICISMS of the positivistic approach to knowing and of the divided field of knowledge in modern thought, Dr. Schaeffer is intending to impugn the basic modern presupposition yielding these two epistemological orientations—that the universe is a closed system of cause and effect. This closed system presupposition is the epistemological counterpart of the impersonal beginning presupposition considered and rejected by Schaeffer in the metaphysical formulation of his overall apologetic approach, which I am presenting as a tripartite argument from design. In his epistemological argument, he is offering a presuppositional disjunction (an "either/or": a choice between either the Christian presuppositional "open universe," or the non-Christian presuppositional "closed universe") and calling for a choice based on the ability of each to adequately account for the activity of human knowing, humans being what they are, and their physical environment being what it is—an argument from design. He writes, "What I urge people to do is to consider the two great presuppositions— the uniformity of natural causes in a closed system and the uniformity of natural causes in an open system, in a limited time span—and to consider which of these fits the facts of what is."[1]

Some of the epistemological problems attending the closed system presupposition have been presented and developed. Schaeffer maintains that this presupposition does not adequate-

56

ly account for the human activity of knowing. He then offers the other side of the disjunction, the presupposition of the uniformity of natural causes in an open system, as the one which better accounts for knowing. This open system presupposition is the epistemological counterpart of the personal beginning in his metaphysical argument. Once the universe is considered as not naturalistic, as not closed, the question must be asked: to what is it open? In simple terms, it could be said that what seems to be needed is some kind of Ultimate Epistemological Guarantee or Guarantor, guaranteeing that men can *really* know what they think they know, thus providing a basis for knowledge.

In this formulation of an argument from design, the design of the universe in regard to knowers and objects of knowledge can bring us to some important conclusions. Unless there is some kind of foundational epistemological Guarantee or Guarantor, all men are in a very problematic situation which seems to pull the individual toward conclusions of radical skepticism and personal alienation from all that surrounds him. In a naturalistic or closed universe, there is no such guarantee. However, all men act as if there were a guarantee. Even the radical philosophical skeptic has sufficiently accurate knowledge of things to be able to use a pen and paper to express his views. As long as he is alive, his moving about in his environment requires some accuracy of knowledge. The very success of human activity requires a prior and simultaneous success of human knowledge in terms of correspondence. The conclusion that this is not explainable in a closed universe leads directly to the consideration of the other presuppositional possibility—that the universe is an open system.

Once again, the argument from design cannot lead directly from the data being considered to the specific orthodox Christian presuppositions being put forth by Schaeffer. There are of course infinitely many possible kinds of open universe and epistemological Guarantees or Guarantors which could be postulated to adequately account for the data. An argument from design cannot itself sufficiently adjudicate between these possibilities, and thus cannot lead all the way to any particular one. In his epistemological discussions, Dr. Schaeffer seems to be somewhat aware of this. Unlike his metaphysical formulation of the design argument, in which the Christian presuppositions were presented with the tone of certain, necessary conclusions of the argument, in presenting his epistemological answer, Schaeffer is proceeding in a different manner. After pointing out the data to be considered and the problems to be solved, he presents his set of orthodox Christian presuppositions as a specific type of open system which, *if true,* would adequately explain the data and answer the problems.[2] Colin Brown observed, "Schaeffer's approach may be compared with a set of hypotheses in science. In the first instance, a hypothesis presents an unproved theory designed to account for something hitherto not understood. A good hypothesis is one which makes sense of the observed facts and takes into account the maximum number of other observed facts."[3]

This presentation seems to recognize the values and limits of an argument from design. However, Schaeffer's failure to mention the possibility of other specifications of the open system which would be contrary to his, and his failure to identify his argumentative direction, allow him to make an unwarranted move. He moves from "if Christianity is true, then there are answers" to "therefore, Christianity is true." The logical gap between possibility and necessary actuality has, in this move, been jumped unwarrantedly as it was in the metaphysical argument. There may be an argument which would justify Schaeffer's repeated move from Christianity as a reasonable presuppositional scheme or interpretation of life, to Christianity as the one true world view, although none is specifically articulated by him. If Christianity were shown to be a possible (or reasonable) philosophical position in every area of human concern or experience (none of which demanded a contrary or contradictory position as necessary to be held) except in one area where it was the exclusive, necessary, philosophically explanatory position demanded by the data of that area, then with certain assumptions concerning the unified nature or relatedness of the various areas of human experience, it could be argued that a move from possibility to exclusive necessary actuality in all those other areas would be warranted. Dr. Schaeffer has not compellingly shown any area of necessity, and thus may not yet validly avail himself of such a move.

In presenting the orthodox Christian specification of the open system presupposition as that which has the greatest epistemologically explanatory power, Schaeffer declares that "Christianity has no problem of epistemology. . . ."[4] To explicate and support this claim, he refers to the historic orthodox view of Divine revelation:

> In the Reformation and the Judeo-Christian position in general, we find that there is someone there to speak, and that he has told us about two areas. He has spoken first about himself, not exhaustively but truly; and second, he has spoken about history and about the cosmos, not exhaustively, but truly. This being the case, and as he has told us about both things on the basis of propositional, verbalized revelation, the Reformation had no nature and grace problem. They had a unity, for the simple reason that revelation spoke to both areas, thus the problem simply did not exist.[5]

Dr. Schaeffer's view of propositional, verbalized revelation will not be examined fully, but a few remarks are necessary. If God has spoken to man *about* himself and *about* nature, then revelation can be said to unify both areas of grace and nature, meaning and mechanics, the upper and lower stories. However, Schaeffer offers no argument that revelation "about" (propositional revelation) is necessary as an epistemological base. It is conceivable that the mere awareness of God (nonpropositional revelation) and the intimation of what Divinity entails could result in epistemological solutions from a Christian perspective. Schaeffer would apparently reject such a suggestion, but in his writings does not consider it. I am not advocating this suggestion as a better alternative to Schaeffer's solution but am merely pointing out that an alternative position is possible. It might be equally adequate to the specific problem being answered by Schaeffer. Again, an oversight in Dr. Schaeffer's argument must not be said to weaken the orthodox position but only to weaken his own argument for that position.

In proposing the Christian epistemological base to be propositional, verbalized revelation, Schaeffer does not argue its necessity but its possibility. Once this possibility has been granted, he aims to commend its acceptance as true by demonstrating the many desirable results in terms of epistemological guarantee and explanation which would clearly flow from its actuality. Before presenting an argument to establish this possibility, he points out that in a universe which is a closed system, the idea of revelation is, of course, nonsense.[6] However, with this, he reminds his reader of the problems attending the closed system presupposition, which has been shown to be epistemologically inadequate, and begins his argument from the alternative open system presupposition.

Schaeffer first discusses man as the verbalizer and cites this human ability or activity as the main distinction between man and nonman.*[7] With this first basic datum, he rapidly presents the Christian specifications of the open system presupposition, pointing out their adequate explanatory power in its regard, and moving directly into his argument for the possibility of propositional, verbalized revelation. A rather lengthy quote will help to represent the flow of his argument.

> It [Christianity] begins with a God who is there, who is the infinite-personal God, who has made man in his image. He has made man to be the verbalizer in the area of propositions in his horizontal communication to other men. Even secular anthropologists say that somehow or other, they do not know why, man is the verbalizer. You have something different in man. The Bible says, and the Christian position says, "I can tell you why: God is a personal-infinite God". There has al-

*He refers to the anthropological shift from tool making to verbalizing as the distinctive human mark.

ways been communication, before the creation of all else, in the Trinity. And God has made man in his own image and part of making man in his own image is that man is the verbalizer. That stands in the unity of the Christian structure.

Now let us ask ourselves this question: In the Christian structure, would it be unlikely that this personal God who is there and made man in his own image as a verbalizer, in such a way that he can communicate horizontally to other men on the basis of propositions and language—is it unthinkable that this personal God could or would communicate to man on the basis of propositions? The answer is no. . . . If God has made us to be communicators on the basis of verbalization, and given the possibility of propositional, factual communication with each other, why should we think he would not communicate to us on the basis of verbalization and propositions? In the light of the total Christian structure, it is totally reasonable. Propositional revelation is not even surprising, let alone unthinkable, within the Christian framework.[8]

After postulating biblical revelation as the source of the Christian epistemological answers, Schaeffer begins to enumerate those answers, showing how the Christian presuppositional system accounts for all the aspects of epistemology left unexplained and problematic by the closed system presupposition. First of all, the Christian epistemology provides for reality in its first move. "In epistemology we know the thing is there because God made it to be there. It is not an extension of his essence, it is not a dream of God as much Eastern thinking says things are. It is really there."[9]

Second, Schaeffer has presented the problem of correlation in this way:

The fact is that if we are going to live in this world at all, we must live in it acting on a correlation of ourselves and the thing that is there, even if one has a philosophy that there is no correlation. There is no other way to live in this world.[10]

He specifies the Christian answer, also a Guarantee because of the Guarantor:

The God who is there made the universe, with things together, *in relationships.*

It is not surprising that if a reasonable God created the universe and put me in it, he should also give a correlation of the
categories of my mind to fit that which is there, simply because
I have to live in it.[11]

In addition to the problems of the first move and correlation,
Schaeffer addresses the specific epistemological problem, so
emphasized in this century, of knowing other people and offers
the Christian answer:

Even with a non-Christian, the Christian has some way to begin: to go from the façade of the outward to the reality of the
inward, because no matter what a man says he is, we know
who he *really* is. He is made in the image of God; that's who
he is.[12]

In this quote, "the image of God" refers to those human attributes and aspirations called by Schaeffer "the mannishness of
man," in their real status as created by and fulfillable in relation to, God. The biblical doctrine of the image of God is seen
here as providing an intersubjectively available source for
knowledge of the deepest truths about any man, on which basis
further knowledge can be built. On this basis, the problems
of knowing others and knowing with others can be substantially
solved.

Dr. Schaeffer presents one other, and very important result
of the Christian view of epistemology concerning reality and
the human imagination:

I live in a thought world which is filled with creativity; inside
my head there is creative imagination. Why? Because God,
who is the Creator, has made me in His own image, I can go
out in imagination beyond the stars. . . .
    Being a Christian and knowing that God has made the ex-
ternal world, there is no confusion for me between that which
is imaginary and that which is real.[13]

This is a very significant result of the Christian set of presuppositions. The problem of distinguishing between reality and fantasy plaguing the closed system presupposition, especially because of the divided field of knowledge, is gone. The Christian presuppositions eliminate this problem in two ways. First is the guaranteed created reality of the physical universe, which is truly externally "there." Second, on the basis of the universe as an open system, with revelation uniting areas of meaning and physical existence, logical rational thought (with its personal elements) does not lead to final pessimism concerning the status of man, and is therefore not abandoned in any area of enquiry. Every facet of the individual's knowledge can therefore be related to the body of that knowledge, no conclusion being necessarily isolated from all else; hence, a unified field of knowledge is established, a major step toward distinguishing between reality and fantasy.

To summarize Dr. Schaeffer's epistemological formulation of his overall argument from design, it seems as though he is applying a principle recognized in scientific confirmation theory to argue for the orthodox Christian presuppositional system in reference to the data of human epistemological phenomena. In confirmation theory, if the occurrence of a given event would, on its own, be a great surprise (or highly improbable), but on the basis of a certain theory, completely expected, and that event is observed, then the theory predicting or accounting for it is greatly confirmed. Schaeffer mentions that, to the Christian, various aspects of epistemology unaccounted for by the closed system presupposition are "no surprise."[14] Since the orthodox Christian presuppositional system proposed by Schaeffer does account for the epistemological phenomena being considered and does answer problems attending the major alternative presuppositional scheme—the closed system presupposition—the Christian system proposed can be said to be greatly confirmed. However, this direction of argumentation cannot adjudicate between Schaeffer's system and other possible open system presuppositional sets which could account for the data. Nevertheless, the significant value as well as limitations of this argumentative direction should be recognized. In regard to basic epistemological questions, as well as to metaphysical questions, the orthodox Christian system has been shown to be a reasonable philosophical position within the limits of the area discussed, one which adequately deals with those foundational human issues.

5

The Moral Argument

THE THIRD DIVISION of Dr. Schaeffer's tripartite argument from design is a consideration of human moral phenomena. Here again he compares the two basic presuppositions concerning the universe—the impersonal beginning (or closed system) and the personal beginning (or open system)—in regard to their respective explanatory power to subsume all the data being examined. In three ways, this is a most important direction of theistic discussion for pre-evangelistic apologetic purposes. First, even to those people who seldom if ever consider metaphysical or epistemological problems, moral questions—questions of right and wrong—are familiar as a normal part of life. Consequently, this is a universal point of contact for apologetic dialogue, an important consideration for a Christian apologist whose efforts are motivated by a universal intent.

Second, in an apologetic with pre-evangelistic purposes such as Schaeffer's, there must be a preparatory examination and explication of the human condition apart from the Evangel. This will involve considerations of sin and guilt, the moral problems addressed by the answer of the Christian Gospel. Thus, discussions of moral phenomena are more than merely academically interesting; they are a necessary preliminary and component part of the evangelistic endeavor.

Third, since the work of Kant, the role of moral considerations in theistic discussion has been widely recognized and extensively developed. This has been an important area of theistic argument yielding many insights which can effectively be incorporated into a comprehensive apologetic, even though most formulations of theistic "proof" arising from moral data have been either fallacious, basically unconvincing, or at least ambiguous.

Although this would seem to be an important direction of apologetic discussion, it is the weakest of Dr. Schaeffer's presentations, not because he does not show the congruence of the orthodox Christian presuppositions with the human moral phenomena discussed, and the resultant possibility of their actual truth—he does—but because he claims once again to have demonstrated the philosophic *necessity* of the Christian system being true, after presenting only a group of generalized claims and arguments, most highly disputable if not plainly false, which in no way warrant this extreme conclusion. It will be valuable to examine his moral discussions for the purpose of again seeing how he does show the compatibility of the orthodox Christian presuppositions with a basic area of human thought and experience, but obviously failing to see or appreciate the importance of establishing the possibility of the Christian answer being true, he once more overextends the validity of his arguments and claims such conclusions as "we must understand that this is not simply the best answer—it is the only answer in morals for man in his dilemma;" and "if God is not there (not just the word 'God', but God himself being there, the God of the Judaeo-Christian Scriptures), there is no answer at all to the problem of evil and morals."[1]

Dr. Schaeffer introduces his main arguments from moral phenomena with a presentation of what he calls the dilemma of man: "Man is able both to rise to great heights and to sink to great depths of cruelty and tragedy."[2] "So man stands with all his wonder and nobility, and yet also with his horrible cruelty that runs throughout the warp and woof of history."[3]

His strategy is to take this "dilemma"—the most general moral experience of men—and, assuming that it requires and admits of an ultimate explanation (quite an assumption), to compare the impersonal and personal beginning presuppositions for their respective explanatory power. Before proceeding further, it must first be asked what this basic data, the alleged "dilemma," really is. If it is a description of human behavior which presupposes the validity or applicability of moral evaluative notions such as nobility and cruelty (and further of a standard to which these terms refer), then this very first move would be unacceptable from various philosophical positions which consider such terms finally meaningless. It could accordingly be argued that for a Christian apologist to present such a loaded claim as basic data to be universally accepted is to beg the question. However, if we construe this dilemma to be merely the observation that, in general, men throughout history have viewed their own actions and those of others in terms of both nobility and cruelty, right and wrong, then this can be acceptable as basic data, and the discussion may begin. It must be noted that Dr. Schaeffer does not acknowledge the necessity of such a distinction in his first move. This illustrates the lack of clarity and precision in his arguments, which must be remembered in the ensuing presentation.

Again, Schaeffer first considers the presupposition of an impersonal beginning to the universe as a possible ultimate backdrop and locus of explanation for the basic moral phenomena of men. He asserts that "if one starts with an impersonal beginning, the answer to morals eventually turns out to be the assertion that there are no morals. . . ."[4]

This assertion is never explicated, except with another claim to the effect that, with an impersonal beginning, cruelty is ultimately equal to noncruelty, that "everything is finally equal in the area of morals."[5] He seems to be claiming here that the ultimate unity and homogeneity of being in an impersonal universe entails that there is finally nothing intrinsic to the nature of that universe which corresponds to the moral distinctions customarily made by men. The making of moral distinctions (not particular moral distinctions, but the activity in general), Schaeffer refers to as "moral motions" and identifies this activity as part of the "aspirations" of man, thereby incorporating it

into his concept of the "mannishness of man," or human personality.[6] When moral motions are seen as human aspirations, it
can then be argued, in the manner of the metaphysical argument from personality, that they are unfulfillable in an impersonal universe,[7] which, if true, may be a tragic conclusion, but
which in no way (apart from psychological considerations) renders the impersonal beginning difficult or impossible to maintain.

Schaeffer claims that in a universe without ultimate moral
absolutes or universals (e.g., an impersonal universe), there
are only three possible bases or standards from which or by
which human moral motions can operate: hedonism, sociologi-
cal law, or totalitarianism, all humanly manufactured sets of
moral absolutes. In criticism of the first he says that "hedonism
can function as long as you have one man. But as soon as you
have more than one person in society, chaos immediately follows."[8]

In criticism of the second, which he calls the dictatorship of
fifty-one percent,[9] he suggests that a majority opinion could allow anything to be considered right or just—law by con-
sensus—and that this also could conceivably have greatly undesirable results apart from a nonfluctuating standard of con-
straint. Against the third possibility, a totalitarianism wherein
a minority, an elite, or one man sets up "arbitrary absolutes," he
also suggests the likelihood of undesirable, unrestrained results.[10]

This brief discussion, of course, does not begin to touch the
ethical-jurisprudential questions involved in such claims and
criticisms. These three alternatives have just been offered by
Schaeffer to lead up to a summary such as, "Neither of these
alternatives corresponds to the moral motions that men have,
nor to what men mean when they speak of morals."[11]

Two criticisms must here be made. First, this claim is un-
supported by any argument. Second, even if it were, that there
are only three alternative bases or standards for moral motions

among men in an impersonal universe is not at all evident, but clearly unacceptable. It has of course been argued in various ways over the past century that the evolutionary process somehow provides a framework of moral reference. Basic human instincts could be cited as loci for the moral constraints needed in society. The physical, survival, functional needs of men in society or community could act as moral matrices for the guiding of moral motions. Even the moral argument of C. S. Lewis concludes an "impersonal mind" as the required supernatural locus of moral absolutes.[12]

In summary, it is clear that there are many possible bases or explanations for moral motions in an impersonal universe. They could easily have arisen from evolutionary or community survival needs, for example, and consequently, when identified as a human "aspiration," the practice of making moral distinctions could be said to be "fulfilled" when it is successfully functional within those contexts from which it arose. Although this attempt to impugn the impersonal beginning presupposition is unsuccessful, it does seem to have hit upon something which can lead to Schaeffer's desired result. If it is legitimate to view the practice of making moral distinctions, or perhaps the aspirations which may be behind that practice, as a distinct component of human personality, then moral phenomena can turn us back upon the metaphysical argument from personality. Moral motions would then be one more manifestation of that about man which is incompatible with an impersonal or merely naturalistic universe. Although Dr. Schaeffer does not acknowledge the dependence of his moral discussion on the metaphysical argument for its rejection of the impersonal beginning, he concludes his moral consideration of the impersonal presupposition with a mention of the metaphysical repudiation of it.

Without having clearly shown the impersonal beginning to be inadequate to account for the dilemma of man—the fact that men throughout history have made moral distinctions, and have regarded their own actions and the actions of others both as noble and as cruel—we are asked to consider the possibility of a personal beginning to the universe.* Of course, once again the only personal beginning considered is the orthodox Christian conception of God. If Schaeffer were avowedly attempting only to argue the *possibility* of holding this specific presupposition by demonstrating its ability to both correspond with and explain the data of moral phenomena, it would be permissible for him to so quickly bypass the impersonal beginning and to ignore all other conceivable personal beginnings. However, his claim to prove the moral necessity of the Christian presupposition as the only one which accounts for the data would require an examination and demonstrated negative evaluation of all other possible basic presuppositional positions (of which there are infinitely many), a clearly impossible task. Although his declared argumentative goal is unattainable, it will be valuable to outline Schaeffer's argumentative presentation for the purpose of further seeing both the theological perspective from which his apologetic is motivated, and the manner in which it is presented.

The question to which Dr. Schaeffer first addresses himself is, "If we begin with a personal beginning and look at man as he now is, how do we explain the dilemma of man's cruelty?"[13]

It should be noted that this question and its subsequent answers reveal that Dr. Schaeffer's intended meaning of "the dilemma of man," stated in terms of nobility and cruelty, is that which was seen to be unacceptable from various philosophical positions as plainly begging the question: The basic data to which Schaeffer's arguments appeal in support of his position require for their meaning and acceptance the prior acceptance of a standard of moral evaluation on which the terms nobility and cruelty depend for their meanings and application to human behavioral phenomena. However, unless a certain philosophical position (like Schaeffer's) is already accepted, the existence of such a standard need not be accepted, and "man's

---

*Dr. Schaeffer makes a few other criticisms of the impersonal beginning, none decisive, which will not be mentioned here.

cruelty" need not be explained, because the term can be said to be meaningless.

Schaeffer would reply that a philosophy which maintains the meaninglessness of moral terms such as "cruelty" is not true to human experience. He has already claimed that all men have moral motions, and thus apply moral distinctions, with whatever terms. However, his argument still seems to rely on one particular moral standard—the one to which he refers when he says "cruelty"—and he has argued the universality of moral motions only, and not of his particular moral standard. Nevertheless, we may continue with his argument if it is accepted that, whatever the particular standard applied, there has always been, in every human society, behavior considered wrong or cruel. The question may then be asked why men everywhere have broken whatever standards they have had. If Schaeffer wishes to go further and claim that men everywhere have the same basic underlying moral standard, and have broken it, manifesting universally recognized cruelty or evil, he must substantiate such a claim through anthropological data, a direction persuasively undertaken by C. S. Lewis in *The Abolition of Man,* but a direction questioned by many anthropologists.[14] This seems to be his approach.

Once a general notion has been formulated as to what the term "cruelty" refers, Schaeffer's explanation for the relation of the phenomena involved in this notion to the nature of human personality, supposing a personal beginning, may be examined. He asserts:

> There are two possibilities. The first is that man as he is now in his cruelty is what he has always *intrinsically* been: that is what man is. The symbol m-a-n equals that which is cruel and the two cannot be separated.[15]

From this first explanation, he claims that two problems arise. At this point the presupposition of a personal beginning again becomes further defined, as the orthodox conception of creation is assumed, with its implied "ex nihilo" (creation out of nothing). The first problem is, "If man was created by a personal-infinite God, how can we escape the conclusion that the personal God who made man cruel is himself also bad and cruel?"[16]

This is, of course, an aspect of the traditional formulation of the problem of evil. As illustrations of this problem being understood, Schaeffer cites Baudelaire's dictum, If there is a God, he is the Devil,[17] and Camus' point that in such a world, evil might not be fought or resisted without fighting or resisting God as well.[18]

Schaeffer claims that all modern liberal theology is faced with this problem since it has relinquished belief in "a space-time, historic change in man," or the traditional orthodox conception of the fall of man. He further claims that liberalism (in which he includes neoorthodoxy) extricates itself from this problem by "a step of faith against all reason,"†[19] proclaiming the goodness of God and simultaneously maintaining the continuity of human nature with its evil from the point of creation. Dr. Schaeffer's particular conservative approach to the first three chapters of Genesis as well as his generalized and undeveloped assertions about "liberal theology" raise myriads of problems which cannot be considered within the limits of this study, but any of which may render his argument completely unconvincing.[20] In saying this, I am not intending to disagree with Dr. Schaeffer's views. I am merely pointing out that these aspects of his argument are insufficiently developed or defended to elicit the kind of assent necessary to effectively lead readers through successive stages of the argument to a conclusion which will be generally acceptable on the basis of that argument.

The second problem which Schaeffer presents as attending the view that there has been a moral continuity to human nature, is that with a humanity which is seen as intrinsically inclusive of evil, there can never be "any hope of a qualitative change in man,"[21] and pessimism results. Even within the framework of Schaeffer's own theological tradition there could

†Such a step is claimed to yield all the dichotomy problems presented in the epistemological argument.

be a simple, decisive criticism of this alleged problem. If God is omnipotent, then He can effect *any* kind of logically possible change.

Of course, if the term "man" is defined as "a being which is intrinsically evil," then to make a qualitative change *within* man eliminating evil is by definition logically impossible. However, God's changing man into something other than man in order to eliminate evil is not thereby precluded. The new being resulting from this change could be called "man-in-Christ," with the term "man" no longer defined as intrinsically inclusive of evil. Thus, there would be no problem of ultimate pessimism for the nature of man even though man is viewed as intrinsically evil apart from the transforming power of God. Once again, I am not offering this as my alternative to Schaeffer's position (it is not). I am only pointing out weaknesses in his argument by presenting possible alternatives which he does not eliminate in the course of the argument.

Some general comments and criticisms must be directed toward what Schaeffer is attempting to do with all these claims and problems. He is once again trying to refute or demonstrate difficulties in positions other than his own, to prove the *necessity* of his presuppositional scheme which includes a "space-time, historic fall," or moral discontinuity in the nature of man. As has been argued, such a proof is impossible. In addition to the mistake of attempting the impossible, Dr. Schaeffer has formulated his claims and arguments in such a way that they are ambiguous and problematic. An example of this would be his use of the word "man" as a generic term. His entire argument as to whether there is a moral continuity or discontinuity to "man" assumes many notions having to do with his particular generic view of humanity (presumably arising from such orthodox doctrines as original sin), which he never articulates, and which function as hidden premises in the argument, rendering it unconvincing if not completely incomprehensible to those who do not already share the same notions. He seems to be unaware of what is possible and what is not possible in theistic argumentation. Once again he can be seen to be trying to argue the reader all the way into his own position by attempting to close all other doors. Of the innumerable doors which he would have to close, the ones he can close are pushed mainly by the force of notions which are available only after his position is accepted—the customary circularity of a presuppositional argument. This circularity has a purpose in presuppositional argumentation. If a presuppositional set is being proposed for acceptance, and it can be shown, on the basis of its acceptance, that all the data to be accounted for is in fact subsumed, and even that other presuppositional sets are not as desirable (although this is not necessary), then the presuppositional set in question is confirmed or commended as a possible position which can be held. This is the only presuppositional conclusion attainable—that of possibility. Dr. Schaeffer is engaging in this direction of argumentation, but continues to belie it by his tone, style, and many of his argumentative particularities.

To conclude this presentation of Schaeffer's argument from design based on moral phenomena, the second possible explanation for man's cruelty, presented by him as the specific orthodox Christian formulation of the personal beginning is that "man as he is now is not what he was; that man is discontinuous with what he has been, rather than continuous with what he has been . . . man is now abnormal . . . because he changed himself. Man as he now is by his own choice is not what he intrinsically was."[22]

This is just a way of describing what Schaeffer elsewhere refers to as "the space-time, historic fall."[23] The orthodox Christian, personal beginning presuppositional outlook presented by Schaeffer is claimed to explain the dilemma of man, yielding four results. First, there is an explanation for why man is cruel which does not impugn the moral nature of God (there is no direct theistic moral problem of evil). Second, since the cruelty of man is not intrinsic to what man is, but is abnormal, there is a hope of solution or restoration to normality (this is the point at which Schaeffer brings in the reconciliatory work of Christ). Third, since moral evil is not normal and is not in a directly derivative relationship to God, there is a basis for fighting social evil or injustice without the problem of fighting God. Fourth, the personal beginning—God—can be said to be good "with the total exclusion of evil." So, Schaeffer not only presents the orthodox presuppositions as yielding ultimate explanations for human moral phenomena (the dilemma) but also claims that the results of those presuppositions pose no insurmountable problems but rather eliminate possible problems, in the area of morals.‡[24]

‡It must not be left unsaid that the traditional "problem of evil" is immensely more complex than Schaeffer's discussion indicates. Literature on the subject, from both philosophical and theological perspectives, is vast and illuminating for those who wish to work through it. There is no simple, obvious solution to the problem in all its complexities, although there are avenues (many heavily travelled) in the direction of a solution or set of possible solutions consistent with biblical doctrines.

6

Intentions, Methods, and Results

Now that the structures of the presuppositional arguments formulated by Dr. Schaeffer in the three areas of metaphysics, epistemology, and morals have been examined and analyzed with the purpose of ascertaining both their values and their limits as arguments, some concluding remarks and evaluations concerning the general apologetic intentions, methods, and results of his work will be offered. His intentions will be recounted briefly from autobiographical information, his methods will be related to the basic model of human thought, reasoning, and belief which seems to underlie and generate them, and his results will be evaluated from the perspective of alternate models of thought and the process of coming to believe with which the apologist is often concerned.

APOLOGETIC INTENTIONS

In regard to his own spiritual pilgrimage, Schaeffer relates that early in life he became dissatisfied with the "liberal" church which he had been attending. Concluding that the minister there "was giving answers to nothing," he left as an agnostic. He then began reading philosophy in his "search for answers," and, among other texts, decided "as a matter of curiosity" to read through the Bible.[1] During a period of about six months, he testifies to having become a Christian "because I was convinced that the full answer which the Bible presented was alone sufficient to the problems I then knew, and sufficient in a very exciting way."[2]

The manner in which he saw the Bible as providing him with answers, he describes in this way:

> And I found truth in that Book. In my reading of philosophy I saw that there were innumerable problems that nobody was giving answers for. But in the Bible I began to find answers, not individual answers that shot down the problems one at a time, but a series of answers that bound all the problems together. The Bible, it struck me, dealt with man's problems in a sweeping, all-encompassing thrust.[3]

So Schaeffer came to see the Bible as providing a system of answers and consequently concluded that "Christianity is a system, but it isn't only a system."[4] He specifies further that:

> By "system" we do not mean a scholastic abstraction, nevertheless we do not shrink from using this word. The Bible does not set out unrelated thoughts. The system it sets forth has a beginning and moves from that beginning in a non-contradictory way. The beginning is the existence of the infinite-personal God as Creator of all else.[5]

Dr. Schaeffer's apologetic intention thus involves communication of what he believes to be the content of the biblical system, as revealing the object of Christian faith, in a milieu which gives primacy to the volitional or experiential, often to the neglect of the cognitive, in questions of faith. He found intellectual answers in the Bible and in turn seeks to set forth those answers as both auxiliary and necessary in a full proclamation of the kerygma. He goes so far as to say that "we have to take the initiative to stress that the mind belongs to Christ, the whole man is to come to Christ. In other words, if the cultural and intellectual questions aren't asked when we lecture, then we have to raise the questions."[6]

APOLOGETIC METHODS

Dr. Schaeffer's conception of Christianity as a system has significantly contributed to the choice of his apologetic methods. He puts forth Christianity as a set or system of foundational presuppositions which is to be evaluated as a system in the manner of scientific hypothesis selection or confirmation theory. The Christian system is compared with competing, contradictory systems in regard to their respective powers to subsume and explain all the data of human thought or experience in the universe. However, he often seems to misunderstand the processes involved in hypothesis selection. It has already been pointed out in this study (more than once) that both Schaeffer's argumentative progression and his terminology often indicate an underlying model of human thought or reasoning as a totally dispassionate, disinterested, nonpersonal, mechanical operation. This model also includes the human activity of coming to believe, with the subsequent belief. He gives only brief, passing definitions of rationality or reason as somehow having to do with thinking and acting on the basis of the logical law of non-contradiction.[7] Accordingly, his basic apologetic method is a large-scale application of this particular logical movement. Operating from his three basic assumptions about human presuppositions—that everyone has them, that only those of the orthodox Christian system adequately and completely correspond to and explain both the nature of the physical universe and the way men must live in that universe, and that no non-Christian can be completely consistent to his own set of presuppositions as he lives in the world truly described by only the Christian system—Dr. Schaeffer seeks to find the point at which a non-Christian becomes inconsistent with his own set of presuppositions, the "point of tension," and to "push" the man from that point toward "the logical conclusion" of those presuppositions. He sees the situation of a non-Christian in this way:

> Every person feels the pull of two consistencies, the pull towards the real world and the pull towards the logic of his system. . . . The more logical a man is to his own presuppositions, the further he is from the real world; and the nearer he is to the real world, the more illogical he is to his presuppositions.[8]

The purpose of pushing a man to the logical conclusion of his presuppositions in any given area seems to be to demonstrate the inadequacy of those presuppositions to account for the data of that area. In his metaphysical, epistemological, and moral arguments, Schaeffer moves in the direction of doing this with contradictorily non-Christian presuppositions. He seems to expect the man so confronted to rebound to the antithetically adequate position of orthodox Christianity as the true set of presuppositions, and thus, to believe. One can picture Dr. Schaeffer as throwing a rubber ball against a wall, expecting it to bounce back right into his hands. However, different rubber balls often have different bounces. The human analogue to this must be recognized.

If this overall apologetic application of antithetical movement (the law of noncontradiction) is expected to lead a man all the way to Christ and Christian faith, it must assume an inaccurately mechanical model of human thought and belief which fails to recognize the many tacit, personal, and nonlogical moves necessary in any process of coming to know or believe. Schaeffer himself occasionally reveals some of the personal elements which contribute toward his own evaluation of the Christian system as better than any other, and as true:

> The strength of the Christian system—the acid test of it—is that everything fits under the apex of the existent, infinite-personal God, and it is the only system in the world where this is true. . . . That is why I am a Christian and no longer an agnostic. In all other systems something "sticks out", something cannot be included; and it has to be mutilated or ignored.[9]

> The Christian system is consistent as no other system that has ever been. It is beautiful beyond words.[10]

> Everything goes back to the beginning and thus the system has a unique beauty and perfection because everything is under the apex of the system.[11]

In the comparison of any group of rival hypotheses or explanatory systems, whether scientific, philosophical, or religious, the final selection of one over the others relies on such personal elements as those appreciations of simplicity, continuity, and intellectual beauty which, for Schaeffer, have finally commended the Christian system as true. Regarding this, Michael Polanyi has observed that:

> The affirmation of a great scientific theory is in part an expression of delight. The theory has an inarticulate component acclaiming its beauty, and this is essential to the belief that the theory is true.[12]

Although Dr. Schaeffer in the above quoted passages reveals that his own evaluative and truth functional judgments are made from a perspective which appreciates and applies certain personal aesthetic criteria, he nowhere acknowledges or seems to realize that such criteria must be personally shared by others before they can appreciate his arguments in the same way that he does. In fact, he seems to assume that his own personal contributions to the formal arguments he gives are universally shared and that, because of this, his own evaluative truth functional judgments can be almost automatically or mechanically generated in others.

In contrast to the mechanical model of thought which is evident in Dr. Schaeffer's philosophical argumentation, his ministry as a whole is very nonmechanical. He sees the importance of developing an apologetic for the needs of his contemporaries and of relating his overall strategy to individuals, as evidenced by the years of personal discussions and dialogues which have taken place at L'Abri. He stresses the lordship of Christ over the whole man, and thus gives great attention to the arts, and culture in general. Another important aspect of his ministry is his concept of Christian community and the development of a creative Christian lifestyle. In all these ways his work has been very innovative within the evangelical tradition, and has evidenced that he sees human personalities as more than logic calculators. After reading and studying Schaeffer's writings and learning of the particulars of his ministry, one develops the impression that although he really recognizes the personal, non-logical elements which make up human thought, belief, and living processes, he hesitates to acknowledge the vital significance of such personal factors in argumentation and philosophical discussion for fear of loosing some type of objective ethos or logical force which seems to accompany the mechanical model of thought.

Apologetic Results

The results of Dr. Schaeffer's major apologetic arguments have been individually analyzed throughout the course of this study. It is evident that he firmly believes the orthodox Christian system to be the only true system of presuppositions available to men. He is also convinced that its truthfulness entails its ultimate philosophical necessity in every area of human enquiry, and presents arguments to demonstrate that necessity. However, there has been shown to be a split between the strong polemical tone and claims of his writings, and the logical force of his arguments. He repeatedly claims to have demonstrated the necessity and consequent actuality of the orthodox Christian presuppositional system, when he has only moved toward showing the possibility or meaningfulness of that system. His arguments fail to accomplish their intended and declared purpose; yet he does not seem to be aware of this failure. The question now arises as to what the relationship might be between Dr. Schaeffer's own evaluation of his apologetic results, and the actual results experienced by a reader or listener of his who might be engaged in a process of searching or of coming to believe. An answer to this question may begin with another question: What is the origin of Dr. Schaeffer's apologetic arguments, and what is their relation to his own history of believing? In Dr. Schaeffer's case, as in every apologist's case (and in every believer's case when he seeks to defend his beliefs), there seem to be only two possibilities. Either he came to believe through the same, or approximately the same, series of arguments and steps which he, as an apologist, presents to others, or he came to believe in some other way, and only after his own believing was achieved did he formulate or take on those particular arguments as his apologetic.

If it is the case that the arguments presented by Dr. Schaeffer are the same or approximately the same as the steps of reasoning which led him to a conviction or certitude of the necessary actuality (i.e., truthfulness) of Christianity, it is noteworthy that he has not been able to present them in such a way that they are universally compelling toward the same conclusion, although he believes himself to have done so. Such a situation is understandable, considering the nature of the process of coming to believe. Schaeffer would have encountered these arguments, or thought through these steps of reasoning within a total context of his own previous life history, his own personal belief tendencies,* and the many other circumstances of his religious or philosophical search. When the formal arguments are presented by him apologetically, they have been abstracted from this web of personal elements which disposed him to see them from a certain perspective, and contributed to his final evaluation of them as convincing, and therefore of Christianity as true. Although many of these personal elements might be communicated or recited by him autobiographically, their total effect on his movement toward and achievement of belief through a particular series of reasoning is not interpersonally transferable. Thus, his presentation of the formal argument, either alone or in conjunction with an autobiographical recitation, cannot guarantee an excitation of the same evaluative response (i.e., a conviction of necessary actuality) in a reader or listener which was, and evidently still is, aroused in him by that argument.

Not only is the total effect of personal elements on overall argument perception and evaluation nontransferable, but the method of formal argumentation can never fully represent or reproduce the process of coming to believe. The personal dis-

---

*"Belief tendencies" would include an appreciation of the previously mentioned criteria of simplicity, continuity, and intellectual beauty.

coveries involved in a progression toward new beliefs are not necessarily logically entailed by prior knowledge or beliefs; and thus strict argumentation cannot alone yield those discoveries. Personal contributions, judgments, and insights must combine with formal argument in a progression to new discoveries or beliefs. Consequently, once a new belief or system of belief has been attained, the process resulting in that belief cannot be retraced by formal argument alone. Accordingly, Michael Polanyi has stated that "heuristic progress is irreversible."†[13] As the heuristic progress in the process of coming to believe yields a change of one's basic interpretive framework itself, or a "change of idiom," another observation of Polanyi's will further elucidate the argumentatively irreversible nature of the process:

> to modify our idiom is to modify the frame of reference within which we shall henceforth interpret our experience; it is to modify ourselves. In contrast to a formal procedure which we can recapitulate at will and trace back to its premises, it entails a conversion to new premises not accessible by any strict argument from those previously held.[14]

Dr. Schaeffer realizes the futility of basing an argument for the truthfulness of Christianity on non-Christian premises, so he argues presuppositionally, challenging basic non-Christian premises or presuppositions alien to Christianity, and recommending their replacement by the orthodox Christian presuppositions. The weakness in his apologetic is that he fails to recognize that predispositions as well as presuppositions must be taken into account; that the transition from one basic interpretive framework or set of presuppositions to another involves an irreversible process composed of personal, as well as propositional or formal, elements. One of his close associates, Os Guinness, comes closer to acknowledging this aspect of the process of coming to believe. Concerning the attainment of Christian faith he writes:

†By "irreversible" he means that such progress is not guided by a fixed framework and thus cannot always be traced back to initial premises (Polanyi, *Personal Knowledge*, p. 75).

> On the one hand between the searching and the believing,
> there is no discontinuity of reason but rather a strong conti-
> nuity so that faith is not irrational or non-rational; on the
> other hand, faith is more than rational in the sense that it is
> rational only to the limits of the validity of reason. Becom-
> ing a Christian is an authentic choice of a whole man; it in-
> volves his reason, his emotions, and his will; in this sense it is
> more than rational.[15]

Although the process of coming to believe is not logically
reversible from the perspective of having achieved belief, it is
recitable. This could be the distinction which explains Dr.
Schaeffer's mistaken evaluation of his own argumentative results. When he recites merely the formally logical steps or arguments from his own heuristic, irreversible progression to belief, he is presenting, as it were, the bare bones of the process.
When he looks at those bare bones he sees the full body as he
personally contributes the tendons, muscles, and so on, which
for him hold those bones together. He bridges the logical gap
from Christianity as possible to Christianity as necessary by
these personal moves and, not consciously aware that he is making such moves, assumes that his readers see that same full
body. Why Schaeffer can look at his own arguments and see
more than is there is explained by another insight of Polanyi's
(who is here speaking of a parallel problem in science):

> We owe this immense power for self-deception to the opera-
> tion of the ubiquitous tacit coefficient by which alone we can
> apply any articulate terms to a subject matter described by
> them. These powers enable us to evoke our conception of a
> complex ineffable subject matter with which we are familiar,
> by even the roughest sketch of any of its specifiable features.
> A scientist can accept, therefore, the most inadequate and mis-
> leading formulation of his own scientific principles without
> ever realizing what is being said, because he automatically sup-
> plements it by his tacit knowledge of what science really is,
> and thus makes the formulation ring true.[16]

On the other hand, it is possible that the arguments presented in Dr. Schaeffer's apologetic may have been formulated or appropriated by him after having believed, his own progression to belief having occurred otherwise. In *Our Knowledge of God*, John Baillie suggests that:

> Students of the history of philosophy have often confessed that the massive and often passionate assurance of God's reality which has been professed by a majority of its leading figures did not really rest upon the arguments which they so painstakingly contrived for the establishment of his existence, these arguments being rather in the nature of afterthoughts, subsequent to their belief in him rather than the cause of it. . . .[17]

Baillie is arguing for the immediacy of the knowledge of God; that this knowledge is experienced apart from argument, but through the confrontation with, or personal revelation of, God in Christ. From Dr. Schaeffer's brief autobiographical references, it is evident that he was first brought to a firm conviction of the truth of Christianity from seeing in the Bible a system of answers to his philosophical problems. Thus, it would seem that the element of argumentation is inextricable from his awareness of God in Christ. However, from Baillie's perspective, it could be argued that the biblical answers or arguments precipitating Schaeffer's conversion did not bring about his first awareness of God but rather only served to articulate and intellectually assure him of the Truth he already felt directly. If the arguments received or conceived then were the same or approximately the same as the ones now presented in his apologetic, then we are back in our first discussion, with the felt Truth being one of the major personal contributions of Schaeffer to the arguments. However, if, as this second discussion is supposing, the arguments that Schaeffer went through in his own progression to belief were totally different from those which he presents in his apologetic, or if he came to believe through no arguments at all, the question must be asked as to why he chose to either appropriate or formulate those particu-

lar arguments which now constitute his apologetic, believing
them to demonstrate the necessary actuality of Christianity (the
orthodox Christian presuppositions) when they do not, but
only move toward establishing its possibility or meaningfulness.

This case would be much like the one before, in that Dr.
Schaeffer's mistaken evaluation of his argumentative results
again would be caused by the perspective from which he sees
the arguments, and the personal elements which he contributes
to them in his mind. These arguments would have been appropriated or formulated after he had already discovered that
Christianity was true. Polanyi offers the simple insight that
"Having made a discovery, I shall never see the world again as
before. My eyes have become different; I have made myself
into a person seeing and thinking differently."[18] In a footnote,
Polanyi mentions "the illusion of 'You can't miss it,' " which
has an illuminating application to the problem of Schaeffer's
arguments:

> Persons very familiar with a district are the worst at giving
> directions to a stranger. They tell you "just to keep going
> straight on", forgetting the forks at which you will have to
> decide which way to go. They cannot realize that their indi-
> cations are altogether ambiguous, because to them they are
> not. So they say confidently, "You can't miss it".[19]

This seems to be equivalent to Schaeffer's repeated claim to
have demonstrated the necessity of the orthodox Christian presuppositions.

PART 2

*The Justification and Formulation of
Christian Apologetics*

7

The Justification of Apologetic Argument

IN THE FOLLOWING CHAPTERS I will attempt to give a justification of the general apologetic enterprise in which Dr. Schaeffer and I are involved. In doing this I will also suggest how insights may be appropriated from Dr. Schaeffer's work and may be applied to a more full and complete apologetic presentation of the truth of Christianity. To do so, I will consider and answer two basic objections. The first objection I will address is the currently popular claim that religious belief is not the sort of thing which admits of formal argument and that, consequently, all attempts to argue the truth of Christianity are at most only philosophical curiosities, completely irrelevant to actual Christian faith. I will suggest, in reply, that authentic Christian faith does involve believing that certain claims about God, man, and the universe are true; and hence that faith is so constituted that at least in some cases one of the factors which, humanly speaking, bring it to fruition can be formal apologetic argumentation. I will then attempt to sketch out a rough description of how it is that formal arguments can enter into the process of coming to believe as a Christian, and thus how apologetics can have a place in evangelism, the proclaiming of Christ.

The second objection which I will consider is the following. Since the kind of argument which has been engaged in by Schaeffer and analyzed in this study can, according to the present analysis, compellingly argue only for theism as against atheism or naturalism, but not specifically for Christianity as against any other theistic religion, it is not really helpful for specifically *Christian* purposes such as evangelism. Granted that argument can have a role in the attaining of Christian faith, and thus in evangelism, how can *this kind* of argument have that role? To answer this objection I will first recall the conclusions convincingly reached by Dr. Schaeffer's argumentative direction and show how these conclusions are related to specifically Christian claims. I will then sketch out how such a relation—that of confirmation—can be the key to all of Christian apologetics; and thus how we can, beginning with what we have learned from Dr. Schaeffer, have a firm grasp on how our faith can be presented and defended in a convincing and rational manner.

In the previous chapter I had begun to consider various aspects of the relationship between formal apologetic argumentation and personal religious belief. From a look at Dr. Schaeffer's apologetic intentions, methods, and results, we have seen that formal argument alone is not sufficient for effecting a specific type of new religious belief, such as Christian conversion, in a person's life. Furthermore, it is clear that formal argument is not necessary for the attaining of Christian faith. It has been suggested that a conversion experience occurs within a complex context of personal factors. I am arguing that one of those factors might well be hearing or having heard arguments such as Dr. Schaeffer's, and that consequently the apologetic enterprise in which he and I both are engaged is justifiable as being relevant to the process of coming to believe as a Christian.

However, there are many philosophers and theologians who currently maintain not only that formal argument is insufficient alone, and often unnecessary, in bringing about a specifically Christian religious belief, but that the whole enterprise of pointing to evidences and giving arguments is inapplicable and totally out of place where religious belief is concerned. To give an oversimplified but roughly accurate explanation, this is often because they categorize "religious belief" as exclusively a belief *in,* rather than also as a belief *that.* Belief *in* is described as an attitude or disposition of trust; whereas belief *that* is said to be assent to the truth of a proposition (assertion or claim). The former is referred to by the term *faith* and is said to be the exclusive domain of religion. The latter is in no way identified or involved with religious belief or faith. Such thinkers would stress the predispositional to the exclusion of the presuppositional, orientations to the exclusion of propositions, as being the operative factors in any process of coming to have a religious belief. To this way of thinking, Christian faith is only an orientation toward life or a way of living, not also a set of beliefs *about* the universe, the existence and nature of God, and the life of man. It is just one particular religious posture which any person may or may not choose to assume. To this mindset, not only can Christianity not be proved, it should not even be argued. Consequently, apologetics (giving a presentation or defense of the truth of Christian claims) is seen as a completely mistaken activity.

Dr. Schaeffer has characterized this perspective on religious belief by means of his "divided field of knowledge" concept, labelling such thinkers as "upper story" men. I do not plan to either rehash or dispute his survey of such positions here but will merely offer my own justification of the apologetic enterprise in which he and I are engaged, with reference to such foundational objections as these men propose. It is important to consider how apologetic arguments can affect people's lives. Unless formal argument can play a role in leading people to Christ and in supporting their faith, we are only playing games with our philosophical maneuvering and ought to see it as such. In response to the entire preceding study and critique of Schaeffer's apologetic arguments, such philosophers would say to me, "Well, Mr. Morris, you have walked into the house that Francis built and have inspected it closely, pointing out weaknesses in the beams, problems in the foundations; you have shown where the paint is peeling off; but we have news for you, the whole house is built on the San Andreas fault and no matter what minor adjustments you make, the whole thing is going to collapse." So, my critique of Schaeffer may even be interesting, but to this way of thinking it is completely fruitless. I have obviously not rejected apologetics as such, and so no matter what I do, I am just tinkering away at a condemned building. So the criticism goes.

Now it must be made clear that such opinions as these are not the domain of antagonists of Christianity. In fact most, if not all, antagonists will want to maintain along with the historically orthodox Christian that evidences, reasons, and arguments are crucially relevant to Christian faith, but of course they will do so for the purpose of arguing against the Christian, that his faith is based on or involves beliefs that are not justified.* Traditionally, Christians and non-Christians, when in dialogue, have met on the same battlefield—they both have assumed that they could discuss reasons for or against holding particular articles of religious belief to be true, and consequently have formulated arguments and cited evidences for that purpose.†

However, with the work and influence of David Hume, Immanuel Kant, Charles Darwin, and others, some shots were fired at the traditional arguments for the existence of God which seemed to many to have obliterated the apologetic arsenal of the Christian camp. Being overwhelmed by the shock of such philosophical and scientific criticisms, and feeling that the basic articles of belief which they still knew to be true could no longer be proved or even defended by formal argument, many Christian theologians denied the very relevance of philosophical, scientific, and historical argumentation to religious

---

*Technically speaking, only a proposition (assertion, claim, statement, sentence) can be true or false. A belief is said to be justified or not justified with reference to both the truth or falsity of the proposition believed and the evidence on which the believer bases his belief. Such propositions will often be referred to as "articles of belief." Whenever "truth" is predicated of a "belief," what is being referred to technically is the truth of the article of belief—the proposition believed.

†Jesus pointed to the evidence of His "works" as bearing witness of Him (e.g., Jn 10:25, 37; 15:24). From Peter's address at Pentecost, through many other speeches and conversations of the apostles as recorded in the book of Acts, empirical evidence and reasoned argument were given a crucial and central role in the proclamation of the Gospel. Throughout most of church history, it has been assumed that the Christian message can be discussed logically and rationally, that it makes claims and has implications whose truth can be argued.

faith, thereby retreating into an impregnable fortress where their faith could be maintained safely without challenge.

Thus it has been not antagonists but some protagonists of the Christian proclamation who have repudiated the possible functions of formal argumentation as properly entering into the process of achieving and maintaining Christian faith. I do not offer this observation as a piece of documented intellectual history but only as a possible insight into the theological mind-set which rejects apologetics as a completely wrong-headed activity. Such theologians are like credulous gardeners who, being told by respected neighbors that their prize plants cannot grow in their present soil, uproot them and take them indoors for protection where they subsequently die from lack of light.

The kerygma, the Gospel, is rooted in history as it was, makes claims about man and his environment the universe as it is, and proclaims the future summation of all things as it will be. The claims of Christ, the claims which have been made by the Church about Christ, and the content of the biblical revelation are either cognitively meaningful or meaningless. If meaningful, they are either true or false. Even if arguments and evidences could never conclusively prove or disprove the meaningfulness or truth of Christian assertions and beliefs, as long as there are believed assertions or propositions implied by Christian faith, argumentation is at least relevant in presenting and evaluating the truth value of those assertions.

Of course those who shun apologetic argumentation hold that Christianity is not a philosophy or a set of propositions to be proved, but is a lifestyle, a way of looking at life which has great powers of illumination and fulfillment for the faithful. Certainly it is evident that Christian faith is not reducible to merely a set of believed propositions or "beliefs-*that*" (belief *that* there is a God, belief *that* God was in Christ, etc.) but is rather a total life response of trust and obedience toward God in Christ by the one who is a Christian. However, the admitted powers of illumination and fulfillment that Christian faith does bring are at least partly the results of its own particular assertions *about* the world.

Its characterizations of life ring true to the believer. Its prophetic promises correspond to the deepest yearnings in the hearts of men. The responses of trust and obedience are only possible, in fact are only meaningful, in the context of propositional knowledge—knowledge *about* who and what is to be trusted, knowledge *about* who and what is to be obeyed. I do not intend to discuss here to what extent Christian faith is existential or personal encounter, and in what measure it is the acceptance of particular propositional claims as true. I am merely suggesting that on close examination, it will be found that Christian faith does involve the acceptance and personal appropriation of certain beliefs as justified (and, by implication, of certain assertions about God, man and the world as true) and that this renders the activity of finding reasons, citing evidences, and formulating arguments in support of those beliefs relevant to the process of coming to believe as a Christian and of maintaining and appreciating that belief once held.

If the general type of apologetic enterprise in which Dr. Schaeffer and I are both involved is justified, then I should be able to give a coherent description of how apologetic arguments logically can enter into a person's attainment of Christian faith. I have suggested that Dr. Schaeffer's arguments function in such a way that their overall thrust can be described by a model of confirmation or probability theory such as is operative in scientific hypothesis selection. On the basis of its explanatory powers in various areas of human experience, it has been argued in this study that theism, and hence Christianity, is confirmed relative to its contradictory alternatives (all atheisms or naturalisms). In my concluding remarks I will sketch out how arguments may be formulated to confirm the Christian position relative to its contrary alternatives (all other theisms) as well. The question almost raises itself: to whom do these arguments constitute confirmation; that is, how do (or can) such arguments function in the lives of real people, if they are not merely philosophical curiosities?

I have maintained that a conversion experience occurs within a complex context of personal factors, each of which contributes in some way toward the final assessment and appropriation of Christianity as true. I will now suggest that, at least in some cases, the way in which those various factors (including formal apologetic arguments) contribute toward the result of Christian faith can be described in the language of confirmation theory by a model of cumulative probabilities. If I can show how this is so, then I will have shown how any apologetic arguments which tend to confirm Christian claims (such as Dr. Schaeffer's) can enter into the process of coming to believe, effect the lives of real people, and be of important use in modern evangelism. To explain what I mean by such a description, I will first review some of the rudiments of confirmation theory and my use of the term "probability" as they are relevant here.

Ultimately, we can say that every hypothesis which is meaningful is either *true* or *false.* When we speak of hypotheses as more or less *probable,* we do so from the perspective of limited knowledge. When we say that an hypothesis is probable—or, synonymously, that it is probable that a certain hypothesis is true—what we mean is that, although we do not know with certainty that it is true, the evidence we have seems to indicate that it is. When evidence indicates the truth of an hypothesis, we say that the evidence confirms the hypothesis. A symbolic example will show how it is that evidence confirms one hypothesis relative to another.

Suppose we have two rival hypotheses, H_1 and H_2, and the description of a possible event E which is of such a type that it would be expected to occur if H_1 were true, but not if H_2 were true. Suppose also that E is observed to occur. That observation is said to confirm H_1 relative to H_2, or to be evidence that H_1 is the true hypothesis. The observation of E makes it more probable to us that H_1 is true. In short, among rival hypotheses, a relevant observation confirms that hypothesis which would render it most likely to occur, which would be the most consistent with it, and which would best explain it. Such confirmation increases for us the probability that the hypothesis which is confirmed is true.

Now, likewise, suppose that there are many events E_1, E_2, E_3, etc., which are such that they would be expected to occur if H_1 were true. They are each more consistent with H_1 than with H_2, and are better explained by H_1. Suppose also that, over a period of time, separately and in groups, many of them are observed to occur. The first observation, say of E_1, confirms H_1 and thus makes it more probable, to however small an extent. Then, when E_2 is observed, it also confirms H_1 and gives it a greater probability, however slight. In addition to each observation's confirming H_1 and individually giving it a higher probability, the effect of all the observations taken together gives H_1 a cumulative confirmation, and thus a cumulative probability that it is much more likely (probable) that H_1 is true than that H_2 is. In this case the cumulative probability has led us to believe that H_1 is true.

A simple illustration of what has just been presented symbolically may be helpful. Suppose we are in a windowless room and we are considering two rival hypotheses: It is raining outside and It is sunny outside. There are many events that would be expected to occur if the rain hypothesis were true, but not if the sun hypothesis were true, such as: water beating on the roof, a friend coming in soaked, water running in the street, etc. Suppose we hear the sound of water beating on the roof (an observation of one of the above events). This observation confirms and raises the probability of the rain hypothesis. Do we then *know* that the rain hypothesis is true, that it is raining outside? No, because it may be sunny outside, but someone is hosing water onto the roof. Likewise, suppose that we see a friend enter the room soaking wet. This observation also confirms and raises the probability of the rain hypothesis, but neither does it prove conclusively that it is true. The man with the water hose could have drenched him. Finally, suppose that we hear the sound of passing cars on wet pavement. This would also be a confirming observation, but again not alone decisive, since it may be that the city street sweeper has just washed the street, and the weather itself is beautifully sunny. Although no one of the above observations would conclusively prove that it is raining outside, their cumulative effect would be to raise the probability of the rain hypothesis so high that we would be fully justified in believing that it is raining outside. This belief can be said to be a justified subjective response to and result of the cumulative probability given to the rain hypothesis by the three confirming observations.

Of course, in day-to-day living, we do not go through such a formal procedure of consciously making and categorizing observations for which we consider rival explanations, just to decide whether it is raining outside. But we do naturally react to the individual and cumulative effects of sights and sounds (etc.) in determining what is and what is not going on around us in our environment (broadly speaking). This is how we live daily. *There is a human capacity to naturally respond to evidences, confirmation, and probability without necessarily ever being consciously aware that this is what is going on.* Such a response is basic to every act of responsible decision making, whether decisions of physical action or of belief. This particular human response is the one which I am claiming is operative in any process of coming to believe something, from the most mundane statement—It is raining outside—to the most exalted religious doctrine—Jesus is the Christ, the Son of God. This is why I am suggesting that the process of coming to believe as a Christian can be described in the language of confirmation theory by a model of cumulative probability. A formal description can be given for what is going on informally, so to speak.

For such a formal description to be possible and to be appropriate for the process to be described, there are two basic requirements. First, since the notions of confirmation and probability apply to hypotheses, it must be possible to treat Christianity as foundationally involving a crucial hypothesis or hypotheses. Second, and correspondingly, Christian faith must involve a belief whose achievement can be seen to be a function of that basic human capacity to naturally respond to evidence, confirmation, and probability which I have just identified. Earlier in this chapter, I argued that the Christian proclamation does involve certain claims about the way things are, and that authentic Christian faith involves believing those claims to be true. Any such claim can be treated as an hypothesis (indeed, the logical status of any such claim can be said to be that of an hypothesis); and, as I have already mentioned, any achievement of belief that a particular hypothesis or claim is true is a function of the capacity to respond to evidence, confirmation, and probability. So it seems that both the Christian proclamation and Christian faith involve elements which are appropriately addressed by the language of confirmation theory and probability.

If it is indeed both possible and appropriate for the language of confirmation theory and specifically the model of cumulative probability (as I have presented them in my symbolic and rain-sunshine examples) to provide a formal description for the usually informal process of coming to believe as a Christian, then it should be possible to conceive of an example in which this can be shown. In fact, an example may make clear exactly what it is that I have been arguing so tediously. Suppose that at a young age a boy is told by his father that there is a God. Suppose also that, while he is growing up, he is not sure whether there is or not, and he becomes skeptical. But during the course of passing years, the situations he experiences, the people he knows, the books he reads, the arguments he hears, and so on, variously affect him in such a way that he begins to think more seriously that the claims of Christianity may be true, that there very well may be a God who has revealed himself to man. If we were to ask him at different times during this period of years what his opinion is concerning the truth of Christianity,‡ his

---

‡Whenever I refer to "the truth of Christianity," I mean the truth of the major biblical claims concerning God, Christ, the nature of man, etc.

answers might be seen to fall into a succession which showed his progress toward belief. We might elicit a series of responses something like the following: "not likely," "I don't know," "maybe," "very well could be," and so on. Such a succession of attitudes would show that it was becoming more probable to him that Christianity is true.

Finally, suppose that he decides that Christianity is true, makes a profession of faith, and becomes a dedicated Christian. From a logical point of view, the process which culminated in his attaining full Christian faith could be described as follows. Each circumstance or experience in his life that had been perceived by him as being more likely to occur, or more understandable, if Christian claims were true than if they were not had individually confirmed to him that Christianity is true. Such experiences as hearing about the answered prayers of a Christian friend, seeing Christian love in action, feeling acutely his own sinfulness and lostness, reading a good argument for the historicity of the resurrection of Jesus, or possibly reading some of Dr. Schaeffer's work, could have had this confirmatory effect for him. These experiences may have perplexed him initially and only later gradually caused him to reflect on what they meant to him. Whether immediately or gradually, consciously or "intuitively," such experiences were in some way seen by him as best explained by the truth of Christianity. All of them together cumulatively raised for him the probability that Christianity is true to such a level that he finally believed it to be true, and with the logical justification of that cumulative probability to which he responded.

It must be remembered that I am not claiming that such a man spent his life calculating mathematical probabilities and categorizing his daily experiences as either "confirmatory" or "disconfirmatory" with respect to Christianity. I am only claiming that there is a human capacity to respond *naturally* to evidences, confirmation, and probability, that this response can be described in the formal language of confirmation and probability, and that the process of coming to believe as a

Christian is at least in some cases an instance of such a response. If these claims of mine are true then I can show how apologetic arguments for the truth of the basic Christian claims can function in evangelism. Any evidences or arguments which can be seen as confirming Christian claims can potentially enter into a process where a response to confirmation is operative. Therefore, apologetic arguments can be among the factors leading up to a conversion experience; and consequently the apologetic enterprise is justified as much more than philosophical game playing, as a ministry which can profoundly affect lives for Christ.

8

Objections and Replies

IN THIS SHORT CHAPTER, I want to deal with some possible objections or reservations concerning this justification of apologetic argumentation. There may be some readers who are slightly unsure about the accuracy of my description of the process of coming to believe. I have claimed that a person can respond to confirmation and probability without ever being consciously aware that he is doing so, that is, without ever thinking in the language of confirmation and probability. But, the question arises, can I consistently maintain both that a person is responding to confirmation and probability and that he is not thinking about confirmation and probability? To put the question generally, can the mental activity of a person legitimately be described by a model which is not consciously being entertained or followed by him? I will suggest that both answers are in the affirmative. It is perfectly legitimate to describe the activity of a person in terms of a model which is not consciously in *his* mind as he is performing the activity. Such a description is not only legitimate but may very well be the best available description of the activity. An example of this would be the act of speaking or writing—the use of language. This use can be described in terms of grammatical rules although the person speaking may not think of a single one while doing so. Nevertheless grammatical rules can accurately describe what is going on. Or take the example of children arguing: "You took the biggest half!" "I did not." "You did too." "Did not." "Did too." Suppose their mother appeared on the scene and asked if they were arguing. She might expect, "No Mom, but he took the biggest half!" Clearly, a model of argument—claim and counterclaim—accurately describes what was going on between the children, although they were not consciously following a plan or method of argument in the manner of trained debaters. The process of coming to believe presents roughly the same situation. In coming to believe something, a person may or may not consciously employ the concepts of confirmation and probability, but either way, the process can be accurately described as a response to confirmation, and finally as a response to cumulative probability.

It still may seem to some readers that belief in God is not the sort of thing that is involved with probability. They may object that no believing Christian, when asked if there is a God, would answer, "It is highly probable." Likewise, it is clear that we as Christians do not go around testifying, "I have trusted my life to Jesus because I believe it is highly probable that He is the Son of God." A person who really believes in God would be more likely to say, "I *know* there is a God" and a Christian to affirm, "I *know* that Jesus is the Son of God." In short, when we take a close look at the true believer, we find that he does not maintain his beliefs as hypotheses which are probably true, but as certainties which he knows to be true.

I will suggest that this is no objection at all to my description of what is going on logically in the process of coming to believe. A person's strength of conviction that a claim is true is his subjective reaction to the claim and may be related in many different ways to its logical status as regards the evidence. Most of us are absolutely convinced about the truth of some claims concerning which we have no direct evidence (for example, "There is a real country named Iceland"). But, in every case of belief there are some reasons for, or grounds of, belief; and even the most indirect evidences (hearsay, rumor, etc.) must have raised the probability of the claim believed to some extent, however small (evidently enough to make it believable).

Evidences that there is a God may accumulate throughout

a person's life until finally he comes to the point where he believes that God exists. This belief can be said to be a justified
subjective response to and result of the cumulative probability
given to "the theistic hypothesis" (There is a God) by the evidences observed. But evidences can never validly bring us all
the way to an absolute certainty that a claim or hypothesis is
true. Confirming observations, or evidence, can logically only
bring us at most to a judgment of high probability as regards an
hypothesis. So whenever we say that we *know* that a hypothesis
or claim is true, or even that we *believe* it to be *true* (rather
than highly probable), we have stepped beyond the reach of
the evidence. To claim, "I know there is a God" or even, "I
believe that Jesus rose from the tomb" is, strictly speaking, to
step beyond the reach of the evidence, but it is a step in the
direction of, and consistent with, the evidence and so is justified
by the evidence.*

It is not the case that only in religious matters do we take a
final step of belief beyond the limits of the evidence. Even in
scientific practice, once a hypothesis has been greatly confirmed
and has achieved a sufficiently high cumulative probability, it
is subsequently used *as true* by the scientist in further work.†
Everyone who is reading these words knows that he or she is
awake and not merely dreaming. But as anyone with an ac-
quaintance with radical philosophical skepticism will tell you,
the evidence you have for such a claim to knowledge does not
certainly and unequivocally prove that you are in fact awake.
In believing or claiming to know that, you have again stepped
beyond the evidence.

I am not claiming here that everyone always steps beyond the
evidence they have to conclude that they "know" or believe
something to be actually true for which the logical status is only
high probability. Indeed the words *probably, possibly, likely,*
and *I would guess that,* and so forth, are not at all uncommon

---

*See pp. 53-55.
†This is just a rough generalization about the attitudes of the average, non-
philosophical, practising scientist who is not at leisure to toy with such sophisticated
theoretical novelties as "the hypothesis is merely a useful fiction."

to everyday language. We usually step beyond the limits of the evidence only in situations where there is good reason to do so: when the cumulative probability is felt to be so great that no further evidence would make a substantial difference, when circumstances demand a quick decision and action, when the hypotheses in question are so trivial and subsidiary to our focal activity (as in the complex web of beliefs according to which we live and move in daily activity) that such a step is the only practical move we could make. Likewise, when a man is considering the existence of God or the divinity claims of Jesus and is led by the evidence to a judgment of high probability concerning their truth status, it is very often, if not always, the case that he will take that additional step to knowing that God exists, or believing that Jesus truly is divine (not stopping with, "it is highly probable that"). Logical probability here becomes personal certainty. In the case of the attainment of true Christian faith, this step is also a deeply personal appropriation of and total commitment to the newly discovered Truth which has been met. In this situation, the factor which has justified the extra step is the active grace of God the Father drawing another to Christ the Son (Jn 6:44). In other words, the firmly convinced belief of the Christian is, in such a case, the result of a logically and evidentially justified process; but at the same time it is also the result of a nonlogical step at the end of that process beyond the evidence, justified by both the direction of that evidence and the supernatural work of God in drawing him all the way to a knowledge—a saving knowledge—of Himself. Thus a personal certitude, or convinced feeling of certainty, concerning the actual truth of Christian claims can be seen to be the justified result of a process which can be described accurately in terms of confirmation and probability, and in which process those claims logically attain at most a status of very high probability.

As I can see it, there may be one last reservation in some readers' minds concerning my description of the process of coming to believe and my consequent justification of apologetics. They may recall that earlier in this study I criticized Dr. Schaeffer for assuming in his philosophical argumentation an overly mechanical model of human thought which did not take into account all the personal contributions of the knower in every act of knowing, or of the believer in every act of believing. Now I have given a description of the human process of coming to believe in language (that of confirmation and probability) which sounds just as mechanical or formal as that which I seemed to fault in Dr. Schaeffer's work. Have I thrown consistency out the window? Am I now committing the same error for which I criticized him? These are questions which I must briefly address and answer before I can expect my justification of apologetics to be completely accepted.

What I have been arguing is that the process of coming to believe, which is usually an informal process, at least in some cases can be given an accurate formal description which will allow us to understand something which is otherwise obscure, namely, how apologetic arguments can be related to Christian belief and faith. What I was criticizing in Dr. Schaeffer's work was not his occasionally formalized or "mechanical" language, but the mechanical model of human thought which seems to underlie his philosophical arguments and according to which that language seems to function. This model is such that Dr. Schaeffer expects certain arguments to prove the necessity of Christian claims and concurrently to elicit an assent from the reader to the truth of those claims. His books often give the impression that any reader, if he is "rational," is expected to respond in a uniform way to his arguments. The reader is shown the inadequacies of certain contradictorily non-Christian positions and is expected consequently to see the necessity of Christianity as alone sufficient to account for the way the world, and human life within the world, is. There is no room allowed for the many personal factors which color and direct any progress toward belief, or any evaluation of an argument as true.

The very claim to have *demonstrated* the *necessity* of the Christian position seems to show that.

My description of the process of coming to believe as a natural response to confirmation and probability is a formal one. It employs formal terminology to elucidate what I have recognized as a normally informal process. However, it is not generated or warranted by, or in any other way dependent upon, a tightly mechanical model of human thought such as that underlying Dr. Schaeffer's philosophical writings. This can be seen in the way it allows for the full operation of all the complexities of human personality and predispositions. The final step in the process of coming to believe, as I have characterized it, is a personal, nonlogical step. Any personal appropriation of a highly probable hypothesis or claim as true is a move which cannot be demanded by logic or "rationality." It is a personal move arising out of personal predispositions and other nonevidential factors. Although justified by the evidence, it is not required by the evidence.

The last step in coming to believe as a Christian is not the only personal move in the process as I have described it. Confirmation is not at any point an automatic, mechanical operation. Whether any given observation is seen as being confirmation for a particular hypothesis is always dependent to some extent on personal factors. Prior beliefs, predispositions, personality characteristics, general physiological and psychological states, and even behavior patterns can influence significantly both the way a person perceives his environment and how he tends to categorize and respond to those perceptions. Thus, a situation, event, or observation which might be taken as confirmation for a particular hypothesis by one man might not be taken in that way by another. The stronger a person's initial orientation is against an hypothesis, the less likely he will be to consider any particular fact to be confirmation of that hypothesis. There are no facts or observations which by nature unequivocally confirm one and only one hypothesis; that is, there is no conceivable event which is not sufficiently ambiguous as to be subsumable under innumerably different explanations. To decide which explanation *best* accounts for a given event and thus which explanatory hypothesis is confirmed by the observation of that event is, in the final analysis, a personal and not an automatic move. This is true of any process of coming to believe which can be described in terms of confirmation and cumulative probability.

A brief example may clarify exactly how this personal element can be operative in matters of religious belief. I cannot conceive of anything which automatically would be perceived by everyone, no matter what his prior beliefs or inclinations, as significantly confirming the claims of Christianity. Consider the following incident in the life of Jesus (Mt 12:22-24, NASB):

> Then there was brought to Him a demon-possessed man who was blind and dumb, and He healed him, so that the dumb man spoke and saw. And all the multitudes were amazed, and began to say, "This man cannot be the Son of David, can he?" But when the Pharisees heard it, they said, "This man casts out demons only by Beelzebul the ruler of the demons.

"The multitudes," however hesitantly, were considering one explanation for Jesus' power to heal; the Pharisees were considering (or rather, propounding) quite a different one. To put it in formal terms, the same event was taken by different observers to confirm two entirely different hypotheses about Jesus.‡

This will be the status of any apologetic argument which we formulate for the presentation or the defense of Christian claims: it will be subject to a multiplicity of different interpretations and explanations; and we will have no guarantee that it will be taken by those to whom it is addressed as confirming those claims for which we offered it. No apologetic argument or "evidence" which we present will necessarily be seen as con-

---

‡Later on, the empty tomb also was subject to a duplicity of explanation (see Mt 28:11-15 and Jn 20:3-8).

firmation of Christian claims.‖ Initially, this is a somewhat
shocking realization. We want to feel that our arguments have
a sort of inherent force in them. We want to be able to demonstrate conclusively, or at least convincingly, the truth of our
beliefs to *anyone*. We have discovered how formal apologetic arguments *can* function in the process of coming to believe, but now we discover that there is no guarantee that they
actually will do so in the life of any particular person to whom
we present them.

Have we then been given the "key to the city" which does not
open any doors? Or do we have a key which fits only those
doors which are already open? In other words, if every assessment of our arguments is entirely a function of such a complex
of personal factors as I have identified, how can we ever expect
to convince the unconvinced? The answer to this question will
show us how we can appropriate the insights of Dr. Schaeffer's
work, incorporate them into a more complete Christian apologetic strategy, and employ that strategy in a manner and with
a humility befitting every activity whose efficacy is dependent
wholly upon the active grace and power of God.

‖This is true of even the most "convincing" Christian argument—a cogent case
for the historicity of the resurrection. Upon hearing such an argument, one listener
may reply, "Aha, this *is* ultimately a chance universe in which even the most
unexpected of things can happen once. A man rising from the dead, can you
imagine that?" Or another may say, "Erik Von Daniken must be right. Jesus
must have been one of those men from outer space, evidently from a planet where
men are so constituted that they come back to life after dying." In neither case
has the data been seen to confirm that claim which it was intended to confirm—
that Jesus is divine, the Son of God.

9

The Formulation of a More Complete Apologetic

I HAVE BRIEFLY described how personal factors decisively influence and direct every step in the process of coming to believe as a Christian. I will now suggest that those factors are of two types: the propositional and the nonpropositional. The propositional factors will be said to consist of suppositions and presuppositions. The nonpropositional factors will be said to consist of dispositions and predispositions.

Constituting the mindset of every person is an ultimate set of foundational beliefs which Dr. Schaeffer has identified as "presuppositions." These are the most basic and the most general beliefs about God, man, and the world that anyone can have. They are not usually consciously entertained but rather function as the perspective from which an individual sees and interprets both the events of his own life and the various circumstances of the world around him. These presuppositions in conjunction with one another delimit the boundaries within which all other less foundational beliefs are held. Such less foundational beliefs or "suppositions" (which I have chosen to call them merely for the sake of syllabic symmetry) make up an uncountably numerous and constantly changing set which, together with basic presuppositions, constitutes the entire propositional side of the complex of personal factors which are relevant to the process of coming to believe.

At any moment, any individual would assent to the truth of

an unspecifiably large number of propositions. This is just to
say that at every waking moment each of us holds a great many
beliefs about the way things are. For example, my own set of
beliefs at this moment ranges from important claims, such as,
"Jesus rose from the tomb" to trivialities, such as, "There is a
light on my desk." This vast set of beliefs undergoes constant
change, incorporating new members and losing old ones. From
every new sight or sound that I perceive, a new belief, however
trivial, is generated. Most trivial beliefs are short-lived—they
are merely forgotten; whereas beliefs of some import are usually
more persistent and long-lived. They continue to be maintained or come to be rejected according to whether they are
confirmed or disconfirmed by subsequent, ongoing experience.

For any hypothesis, claim, or proposition to be accepted by
anyone as a new belief (being added to his existing set of beliefs), at least three general conditions must be met. First of
all, his basic presuppositions must allow for the possibility of
such a belief. If a man's foundational presuppositions exclude
the possibility of a certain claim's truth, then he will not allow
any observations or arguments to count as confirmation for the
truth of that claim. For example, a thoroughgoing atheist,
when confronted with a compelling argument for the historicity
of the resurrection of Jesus, will not allow it to count as confirmation for any claims concerning the divinity of Jesus. If
there is no God, then there certainly can be no Son of God—
so reasons the atheist. He will find another, naturalistic explanation for this strange situation. Likewise, according to such a
man's presuppositions, the universe is ultimately impersonal
and governed by the "laws of nature" alone. So when he hears
Christians reporting miracles and answered prayers, he will
explain them variously as coincidences or pious contrivances.
His perspective determines what he can see and what he cannot see and therefore what kinds of hypotheses he can see as
being confirmed by any given observation or argument.

A second condition requisite for anyone's acceptance of a

claim or hypothesis as a new belief is that he have some reason or basis for holding that particular belief rather than some contrary or contradictory belief. There must be some situation, event, or other observation which can be construed as confirmation or evidence for the truth of that particular claim. This is not a very stringent condition, as a man who is psychologically inclined to believe a certain claim often will respond to the most indirect and minimal circumstance as confirming it. However, for those of us who are interested in convincingly presenting our faith, there are two reasons to attend to this condition. First, it reminds us simply that if we wish to give a persuasive presentation of Christian claims which can potentially enter into someone's process of coming to believe, we must clarify what those claims are, indicate what kinds of things could be taken as strongly confirming them, and finally proceed to supply as many instances of such confirmation as we can. In short, we ought to do our best to provide a substantial reason or basis for believing specifically Christian claims. Second, this condition reminds us again of the importance of presuppositions. If a man must have a reason to believe before he can believe, and if his present presuppositions prevent him from even being able to see any reason to believe, then we must somehow deal with his presuppositions in our attempt to present the truth of Christ to him.

The third general condition which normally must be satisfied in order for a person to take up a new belief is that it somehow must be able to fit in consistently with his other beliefs. We are all much more comfortable when our various beliefs, especially important ones, cohere and are consistent with each other. Paradoxes seem to be an inescapable component of the contemplative life; and so philosophers, theologians, and scientists grudgingly have come to tolerate them. But few ever embrace them wholeheartedly. Even those who do seem to relish and even desirously pursue academic and theoretical paradoxes usually can be seen in their daily lives to be acting according to a roughly coherent set of beliefs. People normally avoid accepting inconsistent or contradictory claims about the world, and thus demand of their beliefs that they hang together as harmoniously as possible.

When a person is confronted with a claim for which there seems to be a great amount of evidence but which conflicts with other claims he holds to be true, he will hesitate believing it. If it conflicts with a large number of his present beliefs or even with a small number of strongly held beliefs, then he will tend to reinterpret all those facts which he had seen as possible evidence for it, and refuse to believe it. However, if the evidence for this new claim is so great that it has for him a higher probability than any of his present beliefs with which it conflicts, then often he will accept it as a new belief and try to revise his other beliefs in such a way that there can be consistency among them. Until this consistency is achieved, he will not be able to see the full import of the newly accepted belief for every relevant area of his life. In fact, it might even be argued that, until some sort of consistency is attained, he merely is entertaining the high probability of the claim and cannot be said to have believed it to be true.

This general condition for new belief—that of consistency—has important implications for Christian apologetics. If we wish to present anyone with a credible case for the truth of Christianity, with the goal in mind of leading him to full belief in Christ, then we must be prepared to speak to more than one area of his life. We must show him that Christian faith is not an isolated religious activity divorced from the rest of life. This can be accomplished fully only by a combination of two things. First, we must proclaim and describe the relevance of biblical truth for every realm of life. We must also show forth in our own lives that relevance. This is not usually considered to be a part of apologetic method, but it is. Only by both hearing and seeing how specifically Christian beliefs can be related consistently to the whole of a belief-set can a man come to understand fully how *he* might believe such claims consistently. In this way, every believer who lives in obedience to God is participating in the presentation of a Christian apologetic.*

Second, we must challenge all the major beliefs that a man holds which are inconsistent with Christian claims. In short, when we engage in formal apologetic argumentation we must use the double strategies of *overwhelming* and *undermining*. We must try to present an overwhelmingly credible case for the truth of Christian claims and we must challenge or undermine any beliefs which would block the acceptance of those claims, presenting through our words and our lives alternative Christian beliefs.

Considering the apologetic potential of our lives—our daily behavior—brings us closer to the nonpropositional aspects of the personal factors which influence the process of coming to believe. I have labelled these factors "dispositions" and "predispositions." The difference between a presupposition and a predisposition should be made as clear as possible. A presupposition is the object of a "belief-that." It is a proposition about some fundamental matter which, although not usually consciously entertained, can be so considered. It can be examined for its ability to account for and explain less fundamental matters. I have claimed that a man's presuppositions function as the perspective from which he sees the world, but that does not mean that he therefore cannot be asked to look at his presuppositions themselves. We can say "Look, you are seeing the world from such-and-such a perspective. There are many things which you are missing from where you are. Step over here and you will have a better view of things." Thus a set of presuppositions can be identified, examined, evaluated, and changed.

On the other hand, a predisposition is not the object of a "belief-that." It is not a proposition about anything. It is more like a very basic personality orientation or tendency. If a man does not tell us what his basic presuppositions are, we usually can infer them accurately from a close examination of what

*See for example John 13:34-35. The work of Dr. Schaeffer and his associates at L'Abri exemplifies this life-style apologetic cojoined with a formal apologetic.

kinds of less foundational beliefs he holds and what kinds of claims about the way things are he will see as possible or impossible. In a roughly analogous way, we can get an idea of what a man's predispositions are, although this process is much less accurate and exact, to say the least. By a familiarity with his general patterns of behavior, his customary range of emotional reactions to certain situations, his inclinations, and even such things as his physiological state of health, his socio-economic circumstances, etc., we can begin to "get a feel for" his predispositions. This, of course, is *the* challenge for psychologists and psychiatrists; and so we cannot expect precise and final results in our nonprofessional attempts to categorize such essential features of the human personality. At best, such inferences as we can make from the various dispositions exhibited by a person daily merely will help us to anticipate how he may react to our arguments, how he may be inclined to respond to our apologetic.

The predispositions and the more changeable dispositions manifested by and influencing a man's behavior will affect his assessment of anything we bring before him as confirmation for Christianity. Exactly how this will happen psychologically, we can neither describe nor predict with much certainty, but from a philosophical perspective, we must realize and acknowledge the importance of these nonpropositional factors in any substantial argument evaluation. The predispositional states of a person will affect practically all his perceptions of his environment. Thus, such factors will be operative in a variety of ways all during any process of coming to believe. Throughout the centuries, philosophical skeptics have pointed out repeatedly that a bad head cold can sway the reasonings of even the most acutely percipient of minds. Consequently, the Christian apologist cannot afford to ignore so influential a factor.

Now that we have looked at some important features of the propositional and, more briefly, the nonpropositional personal factors which decisively influence and direct every step in the process of coming to believe, we are ready to draw some final conclusions and sketch out briefly how our insights may be applied to help us formulate a more complete method of effectively presenting the truth of Christianity to our contemporaries. At the beginning of chapter seven, I promised to answer a certain objection against Dr. Schaeffer's apologetic argumentation. The objection was that, since the kind of argument which he presents tends to confirm theism as against naturalism but does not necessarily confirm orthodox Christianity more than any other variety of theism, it is not useful for specifically Christian purposes such as evangelism—leading men and women to Christ. I believe that we now have a sufficient knowledge of the various factors operative in the process of coming to believe to be able to see not only that Dr. Schaeffer's argumentation is useful for specifically Christian purposes, but that it can be very important, if not indispensable, in any apologetic presentation of Christian claims.

In any complete argument for the truth of Christian claims, both the propositional and the nonpropositional factors influencing our listeners or readers must be addressed. Among the propositional factors, we have already noted the decisive role played by presuppositions in the evaluation and acceptance of new beliefs. Nothing will be seen as confirmation for Christianity by a man who holds atheistic or naturalistic presuppositions. Everything to which we point as evidence for the divinity of Christ or for the truth of any other article of Christian belief will be explained by him in another, naturalistic way. We can understand his inability to see. As we noted earlier, if there is no God, then no amount of argument can show that Jesus is the Son of God. That there is no God, that the universe is ultimately impersonal, that the world is governed by the laws of nature alone—these are the presuppositions we must challenge as the first step in our presentation of Christian truth.

Dr. Schaeffer has drawn our attention to the importance of presuppositional argument. We can appropriate from his work a method of calling naturalistic presuppositions into question. His arguments lay bare the ultimate presuppositions of any contradictorily non-Christian position and show their inadequacy to account for various basic aspects of the way the world, and human life in the world, is. Theistic presuppositions then can be presented as better accounting for and explaining those things over which the naturalist must stumble.

But will not the naturalist merely offer some kind of naturalistic explanation for anything to which we point? Yes, but the whole thrust of our presuppositional argument is that the theistic presuppositions *better* explain certain aspects of the world. They are able to account for certain things more simply and more fully than the naturalist's position. Of course, this cannot be "proved" in any quick, simple, and easy way. The naturalist can either refuse to acknowledge certain things about the world which he cannot adequately explain (such as the reality of human personality), or he can multiply ad hoc hypotheses† to explain those facts to which we point, tacking them onto his presuppositions one at a time. In the first case, we can point out to him that what he refuses to acknowledge in formal argument he cannot consistently deny in his day-to-day behavior, which does make the necessary acknowledgments. In the second case, we can call attention to the complicated inelegance which his position increasingly displays as he attempts to account for what his presuppositions cannot legitimately subsume in a simple and coherent way. In neither case can we force the naturalist to give up his presuppositions. But we may recall a famous historical analogy to his position.

Before the time of Copernicus, the firmly held astronomical hypothesis concerning the heavenlies was that the earth was the center around which the spheres of astral bodies revolved (Ptolemaic geocentrism). Then observations were made which could not be accounted for by the old Ptolemaic system. Such observations became increasingly frequent. At first many who held the geocentric view refused to acknowledge the accuracy of these observations. But as that line of defense became less

---

†An ad hoc hypothesis is one which is made up to explain the event or fact in question and which is not derivatively connected to any larger overall system.

plausible, the geocentrists began explaining each new observation by a new ad hoc hypothesis. The Ptolemaic picture became so complicated and inelegant that its validity finally came to be doubted. The Copernican or heliocentric hypothesis (the sun is the center around which the heavenlies revolve), which some few voices proclaimed, offered an alternative picture which simply and fully accounted for all the observations which so troubled the geocentrists. Thus came about the Copernican revolution.

This is a picture of how our presuppositional arguments may function. We bring observations before the naturalist which he cannot easily explain and all the while hope for a "Copernican revolution" in his life. Whether he will eventually come to see our arguments as disconfirmation for his own presuppositions and confirmation for their theistic alternatives will of course be a function of personal factors, in this case of predispositions—for example, whether he is predisposed to see such characteristics as simplicity and elegance as marks of truth (a certain type of aesthetic predisposition).

When we are contending for the truth of Christianity among people with contradictorily non-Christian presuppositions, presuppositional argument is necessary but not alone sufficient for the accomplishment of our task. We also need to bring forth arguments which can be taken as confirming specifically Christian claims as over against the claims of any other theistic religious or philosophical position. In technical terms, we must offer confirmation for Christianity relative to its contraries as well as relative to its contradictories. Only in so doing will we be offering a reason or basis for holding a specifically *Christian* set of beliefs. Otherwise, we have not given a Christian apologetic, only a theistic one.

To confirm Christianity relative to its contraries, we can apply roughly the same type procedure which we use in presuppositional argument. On the basis of its explanatory power to subsume all the data of human experience—the way the world, and life within the world, is—we can argue that Christianity is confirmed relative to any conceivable contrary religious or philosophical position. How we can go about doing this in the most effective way, I will now outline very briefly. I will not in these remarks present any apologetic arguments of my own, but merely will suggest a *method* of argumentation which best applies various insights we have derived from our study thus far.

The full Christian proclamation involves quite a few assertions about the world. Among these assertions there are both historical and more "existential" claims. Whenever we present one of these claims and support it with evidence and arguments, we are providing confirmation not only for it, but also for the whole of the proclamation of which it is a part. For example, suppose we present the historical claim that Jesus rose from the tomb—the resurrection. Various historical circumstances can be cited as evidence for the truth of this claim. A mass of data can be brought to light which is better accounted for or explained by the resurrection claim than by any plausible alternative claims. Based on this explanatory power, it can be argued that the resurrection claim is substantially confirmed and can be taken to have an evidential status of high probability.

Once it has achieved this status, the resurrection itself then can be cited as evidence for the truth of the Christian proclamation as a whole. The more individual claims we present and confirm in this manner, the more instances of confirmation we will have to offer for the Christian proclamation as a whole. We will be showing that there are in the world many things which are better accounted for, or explained, by the claims of biblical Christianity than by the claims of any other rival religious or philosophical positions. If our individual arguments are well received by those to whom they are addressed, then the many instances of confirmation which we produce may be seen by them as giving to the Christian message a cumulative probability which renders it much more likely to be true than any of its contraries (other theisms).

After all that already has been said about the roles of personal factors in the process of coming to believe, I need not add much here. Of course, any evidence to which we point as confirming Christianity relative to its contraries can be explained in one way or another by those contraries. Once again, as in every step of our apologetic, we depend upon the receptivity of our listener or reader. We depend upon those personal contributions to our arguments which he must make before he will be convinced. That is the reason for a pre-evangelistic apologetic. Before we begin to argue the truth of the Christian message itself we often must engage in presuppositional argument. But that is not to say that we must wait for a man to give up his naturalistic presuppositions and take on theistic ones before we can present specifically Christian evidences and arguments to him. Few men will give up a particular naturalistic stance for an undefined "theism." Our Christian evidences (such as arguments for the resurrection) actually can help to push a man toward realizing the inadequacies of his naturalistic presuppositions, as he is confronted with more and more facts about the world which are anomalous if not completely inexplicable from his fundamental perspective.

It has become clear that the attainment of a full Christian belief-set is a major conversion experience involving the totality of the human personality. From a logical standpoint, it has been called a personal "Copernican revolution," a complete change of perspective on the world as well as of numerous individual beliefs. Such an occurrence as this is deeply rooted in the mysteries of personal predispositions to believe. In our examination of presuppositional argumentation, we have already seen that in a very significant way predispositions seem to be more fundamentally constitutive of the person than any propositional beliefs which can be argued, evaluated, and changed. They in fact determine how arguments are perceived, how evaluations are made, and whether or not any belief changes result. Thus, they are the most important factors in the process of coming to believe.

The very factors concerning which we have been able to say the least—predispositions—are the most important. What an ironic conclusion for the apologetic enterprise. We are shocked into the realization now that we cannot confidently argue people into the body of Christ. None of our arguments carries a guaranteed universal force which can compel every "rational" person to assent to the truth of the Gospel. We are always dependent on something in our listener over which we have no sure control.

But this is no cause for despair. In fact, such a realization leads us into a more biblical attitude toward the values and limits of formal philosophical argument. Jesus said, "No one can come to Me unless the Father who sent Me draws him" (Jn 6:44). We must see that our arguments for the truth of Christian claims themselves can never lead anyone all the way to a total personal belief and faith in Christ. Only the Father can do that. But we are His witnesses, and as such are charged with the proclamation and presentation of His truth, both to our contemporaries and to our posterity. We are to carry out this charge to the best of our abilities, making the most of both our talents and our insights. Herein lies the motivation for developing a considered apologetic method such as that which I have briefly presented. But herein also lies another motivation.

If even the best of our arguments are finally dependent for their effectuality on predispositions over which we have no sure control, we are forced to recognize *prayer* as the most important part of our apologetic strategy. If I argue incessantly for the truth of Christian claims but do not pray for those to whom I address my arguments, I am only a noisy gong or a clanging cymbal. The apologetic presentation of the truth of Christianity is incomplete with formal argument alone. We must argue, pray, and live in such a way that both the things for which we argue and the One to whom we pray are manifested in our deeds as well as in our words.

I hope that this study has been illuminating. As we read the philosophical and apologetic writings of any Christian thinker such as Dr. Schaeffer, we should strive to determine both the values and the limits of his arguments. Only then can we be both appreciative and discerning in our appropriation and use of his work. I have attempted to show that apologetic arguments are not superfluous to Christian faith, but that they can be used by God as vehicles of His truth, operative in the process of coming to believe. However, no apologetic arguments which we formulate or appropriate from any Christian philosopher are ever to be identified with that divine truth. We must never present our arguments as having the same status as the Gospel itself. This is a mistake which has been made too often in the history of Christian thought, and which repeatedly has reaped adverse results. The particular danger resultant from such apologetic self-exultation should deter us from any but the most humble and tentative presentations of any particular arguments:

> When we allow a human invention
> to be confused with Divine intention,
> Or take the current argumentation
> to be equated with proclamation;
> We join a friend with a stranger,
> and thereby always court the danger
> that weakness be found within the new
> and men reject not one but two.

> T. V. M.

Notes

INTRODUCTION

1. Francis Schaeffer, "Why and How I Write My Books," *Eternity*, March 1973, p. 65.
2. Ibid.
3. Ibid., p. 76.

CHAPTER 1

1. Francis Schaeffer, *The God Who Is There* (Downers Grove, Ill.: Inter-Varsity, 1968), p. 179. Henceforth this book will be cited as *GWT*.
2. Colin Brown, *Philosophy and the Christian Faith* (London: Tyndale, 1969), p. 265.
3. Os Guinness, *The Dust of Death* (Downers Grove, Ill.: Inter-Varsity, 1973), pp. 346, 349.
4. Francis Schaeffer, *He Is There and He Is Not Silent* (Wheaton, Ill.: Tyndale, 1972), p. 65. Henceforth this book will be cited as *HIT*.
5. W. V. Quine and J. S. Ullian, *The Web of Belief* (New York: Random House, 1970), p. 8. See also John Baillie, *Our Knowledge of God* (New York: Scribner's, 1959), pp. 59-60.
6. Schaeffer, *GWT*, p. 121.
7. Schaeffer, *HIT*, p. 65.
8. Schaeffer, *GWT*, p. 111.
9. Schaeffer, *HIT*, p. 15.
10. Schaeffer, *GWT*, p. 121.
11. Francis Schaeffer, "Apologetics," tape 6, Farel House Lecture Series, L'Abri Tapes.
12. See Schaeffer, *HIT*, p. 64.

CHAPTER 2

1. Schaeffer, *HIT*, pp. 1-20.
2. Schaeffer, *GWT*, pp. 88, 108, 111. See also Francis Schaeffer, *Escape from Reason* (Downers Grove, Ill.: Inter-Varsity, 1968), p. 30; Schaeffer, *Genesis in Space and Time* (Downers Grove, Ill.: Inter-Varsity, 1972), pp. 57-59; Schaeffer, *Death in the City* (Downers Grove, Ill.: Inter-Varsity, 1969), p. 101.
3. Schaeffer, *Death*, p. 100.
4. Schaeffer, *HIT*, p. 7.
5. Ibid., p. 8.
6. Ibid.
7. Ibid., p. 9.
8. Schaeffer, *Death*, p. 98.
9. Ibid., p. 99.
10. Ibid., p. 97.
11. Schaeffer, *GWT*, p. 89.
12. Ibid.
13. Ibid.

14. See Brown, *Philosophy*, p. 265; Malcolm A. Jeeves, *The Scientific Enterprise and Christian Faith* (London: Tyndale, 1969), pp. 42-43; Michael Polanyi, *Personal Knowledge: Towards a Post-Critical Philosophy*, 1st ed. (New York: Harper & Row, Torchbooks, 1964), especially chap. six.
15. Schaeffer, *HIT*, p. 10.
16. Schaeffer, *HIT*, p. 12.
17. Ibid.
18. Ibid.
19. Schaeffer, *GWT*, p. 95.
20. Schaeffer, *HIT*, p. 13.
21. Ibid., pp. 13-19.
22. Ibid., p. 16.
23. Schaeffer, *Genesis*, p. 58.
24. Francis Bacon, *The New Organon and Related Writings*, ed. Fulton H. Anderson (Indianapolis: Bobbs-Merrill, Library of Liberal Arts, 1960), p. 50, l. 45.
25. Schaeffer, *HIT*, p. 5.
26. Ibid., p. 6.
27. Ibid.
28. Ibid., p. 7.
29. Ibid., p. 26.
30. Schaeffer, *Death*, p. 101.
31. Good, brief summaries occur in John Hick, *Philosophy of Religion*, Foundations of Philosophy Series (Englewood Cliffs, N.J.: Prentice-Hall, 1963), pp. 25-26; and in Ian G. Barbour, *Issues in Science and Religion* (Englewood Cliffs, N.J.: Prentice-Hall, 1966), pp. 71-72.
32. Schaeffer, "Apologetics" tape.
33. Schaeffer, *HIT*, p. 17; Schaeffer, *Escape*, p. 31. See also Jeeves, *Scientific Enterprise*, pp. 9-19; and R. Hooykaas, *Religion and the Rise of Modern Science* (Grand Rapids, Mich.: Eerdmans, 1972).

CHAPTER 3

1. Schaeffer, *HIT*, p. 43.
2. Ibid.
3. Ibid., p. 49.
4. Ibid., p. 50.
5. Michel de Montaigne, *In Defense of Raymond Sebond*, trans. Arthur H. Beattie, Milestones of Thought (New York: Frederick Ungar, 1959), p. 71.
6. Ibid., p. 117.
7. C. S. Lewis, *Miracles: A Preliminary Study* (New York: Macmillan, 1947), pp. 10-24.
8. Schaeffer, *GWT*, p. 44.
9. Schaeffer, *Escape*, p. 34.
10. Schaeffer, *GWT*, p. 178; see also p. 17.
11. Schaeffer, *Escape*, p. 35.
12. Schaeffer, *GWT*, p. 17.
13. Ibid., p. 21.
14. Schaeffer, *Escape*, p. 11.
15. Schaeffer, *Escape*, p. 9.
16. Ibid., pp. 12-14.
17. Schaeffer, *HIT*, p. 43.
18. Ibid., p. 44.
19. Schaeffer, *Escape*, pp. 32-34.
20. Ibid., p. 33.
21. Schaeffer, *GWT*, p. 20.
22. Ibid., p. 21.
23. Ibid.

24. Ibid.
25. Schaeffer, *HIT*, p. 47.
26. This phrase was used by Schaeffer in a question and answer period during the American L'Abri Conference at Covenant College, Lookout Mountain, Tennessee, Spring, 1973.
27. Schaeffer, GWT, p. 22.
28. Ibid., p. 23.
29. Schaeffer, *HIT*, p. 57.
30. Raoul-Jean Moulin, quoted in Francis Schaeffer, *Art and The Bible* (Downers Grove, Ill.: Inter-Varsity, 1973), p. 1.
31. John Macquarrie, *Existentialism* (Baltimore: Penguin Books, Pelikan, 1973), pp. 223-24.
32. Schaeffer, *GWT*, p. 23.
33. Ibid., p. 24.
34. Macquarrie, *Existentialism*, pp. 220-21.
35. Schaeffer, *HIT*, pp. 56-57.

CHAPTER 4

1. Schaeffer, *HIT*, p. 65.
2. Ibid., pp. 76-77.
3. Brown, *Philosophy*, p. 265.
4. Schaeffer, *HIT*, p. 67.
5. Ibid., p. 62.
6. Ibid., p. 63.
7. Ibid., p. 64.
8. Ibid., pp. 65-66; see also pp. 91-97.
9. Ibid., p. 71.
10. Ibid., p. 70.
11. Ibid., pp. 68, 76.
12. Ibid., p. 83.
13. Ibid., p. 85.
14. Ibid., pp. 72, 77.

CHAPTER 5

1. Schaeffer, *HIT*, p. 33.
2. Schaeffer, *GWT*, p. 100.
3. Schaeffer, *HIT*, p. 22.
4. Ibid.
5. Ibid., pp. 22-25; Schaeffer, *GWT*, p. 101.
6. Schaeffer, *HIT*, p. 23. A good example of the moral argument beginning with particular, basic moral distinctions claimed to be universal can be seen in C. S. Lewis, *Mere Christianity*, paperback ed. (New York: Macmillan, 1960), pp. 17-39; and C. S. Lewis, *The Abolition of Man*, paperback ed. (New York: Macmillan, 1965), pp. 95-121.
7. Schaeffer, ibid.
8. Francis Schaeffer, *The Church at the End of the 20th Century* (Downers Grove, Ill.: Inter-Varsity, 1970), p. 33.
9. Ibid.
10. Ibid.
11. Schaeffer, *GWT*, pp. 106-7.
12. Lewis, *Mere Christianity*, pp. 17-39.
13. Schaeffer, *HIT*, p. 27.
14. Lewis, *Abolition of Man*, pp. 95-121.
15. Schaeffer, *HIT*, p. 27.
16. Ibid.
17. Ibid.
18. Ibid., p. 28; Schaeffer, *GWT*, p. 107.

19. Schaeffer, *HIT*, p. 28.
20. See the book review on Schaeffer's *Genesis* in the *Catholic Biblical Quarterly,* 35 (April 1973), pp. 273-74. This review illustrates a common reaction to his insufficiently developed and defended assertions.
21. Schaeffer, *HIT*, p. 29.
22. Ibid., p. 30.
23. Schaeffer, *Genesis,* pp. 85-101.
24. Schaeffer, *HIT*, p. 33.

CHAPTER 6

1. Francis Schaeffer, "Why and How I Write My Books," *Eternity,* March 1973, p. 64.
2. Schaeffer, *Escape,* p. 85.
3. Schaeffer, "Why and How I Write My Books," p. 64.
4. Francis Schaeffer, *The New Super Spirituality* (Downers Grove, Ill.: Inter-Varsity, 1972), p. 27.
5. Schaeffer, *Escape,* p. 91.
6. Schaeffer, *Super Spirituality,* p. 26.
7. Schaeffer, *GWT*, p. 113.
8. Ibid., p. 123.
9. Schaeffer, *HIT*, p. 81.
10. Schaeffer, *GWT*, p. 156.
11. Schaeffer, *Escape,* p. 25.
12. Polanyi, *Personal Knowledge,* p. 133.
13. Ibid., p. 123.
14. Ibid., p. 105.
15. Guinness, *Dust of Death,* p. 358.
16. Polanyi, *Personal Knowledge,* p. 169.
17. Baillie, *Our Knowledge of God,* p. 132.
18. Polanyi, *Personal Knowledge,* p. 143.
19. Ibid., p. 170 n.

Bibliography

Baillie, John. *Our Knowledge of God.* New York: Scribner, 1959.

Barbour, Ian G. *Issues in Science and Religion.* Englewood Cliffs, N.J.: Prentice-Hall, 1966.

Bloesch, Donald. *The Evangelical Renaissance.* Grand Rapids, Mich.: Eerdmans, 1973.

Brown, Colin. *Philosophy and the Christian Faith.* London: Tyndale, 1968.

The Catholic Biblical Quarterly, 35 (April 1973): 273-74.

Guinness, Os. *The Dust of Death.* Downers Grove, Ill.: Inter-Varsity, 1973.

Hick, John. *Philosophy of Religion.* Englewood Cliffs, N.J.: Prentice-Hall, 1963.

Hooykaas, R. *Religion and the Rise of Modern Science.* Grand Rapids, Mich.: Eerdmans, 1972.

Jeeves, Malcolm A. *The Scientific Enterprise and Christian Faith.* London: Tyndale, 1969.

Lewis, C. S. *The Abolition of Man.* Paperback ed. New York: Macmillan, 1965.

―――. *Mere Christianity.* Paperback ed. New York: Macmillan, 1960.

―――. *Miracles: A Preliminary Study.* Paperback ed. New York: Macmillan, 1947.

Macquarrie, John. *Existentialism.* Baltimore: Penguin Books, Pelikan, 1973.

Middlemann, Udo. *Pro-Existence.* Downers Grove, Ill.: Inter-Varsity, 1974.

Mitchell, Basil. *The Justification of Religious Belief.* New York: Seabury, Crossroad Books, 1973.

Montaigne, Michel de. *In Defense of Raymond Sebond.* Trans. Arthur H. Beattie. Milestones of Thought. New York: Frederick Ungar, 1959.

Newman, John Henry. *Grammar of Assent.* New York: Double-day, 1955.

Niebuhr, Reinhold. *The Nature and Destiny of Man.* Vol. 1. New York: Scribner, 1964.

Pascal, Blaise. *Pensees.* Trans. W. F. Trotter. New York: Dutton, 1958.

Polanyi, Michael. *Personal Knowledge: Towards a Post-Critical Philosophy.* New York: Harper & Row, Torchbooks, 1964.

Quine, W. V., and Ullian, J. S. *The Web of Belief.* New York: Random House, 1970.

Ramm, Bernard. *The God Who Makes a Difference: A Christian Appeal to Reason.* Waco, Tex.: Word, 1972.

Rookmaaker, H. R. *Modern Art and the Death of a Culture.* Downers Grove, Ill.: Inter-Varsity, 1970.

Schaeffer, Edith. *Hidden Art.* Wheaton, Ill.: Tyndale, 1971.

————. *L'Abri.* Wheaton, Ill.: Tyndale, 1969.

Schaeffer, Francis. "Apologetics." Farel House Lecture Series: L'Abri Tapes, Tape 6.

————. *Art and the Bible.* Downers Grove, Ill.: Inter-Varsity, 1973.

————. *Back to Freedom and Dignity.* Downers Grove, Ill.: Inter-Varsity, 1972.

————. *Basic Bible Studies.* Downers Grove, Ill.: Inter-Varsity, 1972.

————. *The Church at the End of the 20th Century.* Downers Grove, Ill.: Inter-Varsity, 1970.

————. *The Church Before the Watching World.* Downers Grove, Ill.: Inter-Varsity, 1971.

————. *Death in the City.* Downers Grove, Ill.: Inter-Varsity, 1969.

————. *Escape from Reason.* Downers Grove, Ill.: Inter-Varsity, 1968.

————. *Genesis in Space and Time.* Downers Grove, Ill.: Inter-Varsity, 1972.

————. *The God Who Is There.* Downers Grove, Ill.: Inter-Varsity, 1968.

————. *He Is There and He Is Not Silent.* Wheaton, Ill.: Tyndale, 1972.

————. *The New Super Spirituality.* Downers Grove, Ill.: Inter-Varsity, 1972.

————. *Pollution and the Death of Man: The Christian View of Ecology.* Wheaton, Ill.: Tyndale, 1970.

————. *True Spirituality.* Wheaton, Ill.: Tyndale, 1971.

Swinburne, R. G. "The Argument from Design." *The Journal of the Royal Institute of Philosophy* 43 (July 1968): 199-212.

Trigg, Roger. *Reason and Commitment.* Cambridge: Cambridge U., 1973.